The Cruel Cornish Sea

David Mudd

D1609904

Bossiney Books

First published in 1981
by Bossiney Books
St Teath, Bodmin, Cornwall
Designed, typeset and printed in Great Britain by
Penwell Ltd, Parkwood, Callington
Cornwall

ISBN 0 906456 09 6

ABOUT THE AUTHOR — AND THE BOOK

More than thirty Cornish shipwrecks, spanning four hundred years, have been selected by David Mudd in his fascinating account of seas and a coastline that, in a matter of hours, can turn from the peaceful to the sadistic and — each year — claim their toll of human lives.

Working from newspaper reports, the words of survivors and witnesses, and the pages of official reports, he has turned each incident into a personalised account of suffering and bravery.

As a former newspaper and television journalist, David Mudd covered some of the incidents of which he writes. He admits that it was his experience of the loss of the motor vessel *Darlwyne*, off Dodman Point, in 1966, that gave him the deep concern for maritime safety that has marked many of his activities as Member of Parliament for Falmouth and Camborne since 1970.

'HE GRIEVES RATHER THAN GLOATS'

It was as if the whole village was there, pensioner, child, man, woman, boy and girl. As part of an endless moving chain of bobbing lights from torches, lamps and lanterns, they studded the path from cliff-top to shore looking, for all the world, like a colony of illuminated ants.

On the beach they picked up bottles, cans of vegetables, or crates of fruit. Some of the more adventurous climbed on board the stricken ship embedded on the rocks and towering above them, returning to the safety of the sand with an assortment of 'liberated' articles before taking their place in the line of lights going up the other side of the cove.

As if in answer to my unasked question, the uniformed official who stood beside me, watching, said: "Tis more'n my life is worth, boy, to try 'n' stop'm. They'm only goin' back to 'uman nature. 'Tis instinctive to 'm'.

A fascination for shipwreck is, indeed, part of the Cornishman's character. He grieves rather than gloats; he is genuinely saddened by the loss of a ship and her crew; he is not averse to sharing the spoils that the wreck may give up; but, above all, he holds in awe the combination of the power of the wind, wave and tide that have come together to cause disaster.

Few Cornishmen, if born within a few miles of the coast, will not have a shipwreck featured in their earliest memories. The house in which I was born, in Falmouth, was at the point of a triangle completed by wrecks. To the right, the remnants of the oil tanker *Ponus;* to the left, the unlikely remains of a small group of German

The last moments of the oil tanker *Torrey Canyon* being bombed on the Seven Stones reef in 1967 ▶

submarines dating back to the Kaiser's war.

Ponus went ashore at Gyllyngvase, and caught fire, in November 1916. She burned for three days and nights, her final hours punctuated by a series of explosions of growing intensity. In 1918, the stern was separated from what remained of the rest of the hull but, until well into the 1950s, large sections of the wreck stood out of the sea like some impressionistic sculpture.

Then there were those German submarines under Pendennis castle. At the end of the 1914-18 war, no less than eight of them were sent to Falmouth as targets for gunnery practice. Either the gunners were determined to make their targets last as long as possible, or the undersea craft were unexpectedly robust. Whatever the reason, the fact emerged that, by 1921, only two had actually been sunk.

Perhaps tiring of waiting for their dues, the wind and seas took a hand and, in a winter gale, the six slim vessels were ripped from

Victim of the Lizard November 1911

The *Khyber* lost at Land's End, March 1905

their moorings. With the ease that a bird carries a piece of straw to its chosen place, the gale and tide swept them ashore to lie amidst rocks and crevices to become, for another three decades, a source of interest and adventure to the foolhardy who, until the jagged edges of metal ripped by would-be salvors littered the approaches, found it possible to approach some of the submarines at low tide and clamber over them.

It was my job as a newspaper reporter, and later in radio and television, that brought me more and more in contact with the brutish callousness of the wind and tide, and the inhospitality of the Cornish coast. Ships arrived, like *Janko*, being towed stern-first after having split in two when battered by massive waves twice the height of a normal house. Others, like *Stryx*, looked as if they had made an unsuccessful attempt to get under a low bridge when waves had washed away masts, bridge and funnel with the neatness of someone slicing the top off a boiled egg.

Then there were the ships which called to land the casualties and

Ponus **on fire at Gyllyngvase in 1916**

corpses of violent storms. Men crushed beyond recognition by cascading cargo; others, minus arms or legs, where hawsers, unable to withstand the stress of the storm, snapped and whipped their way through protective clothing, skin and bone with the accelerated precision of the surgeon's knife, but with the gaping devastation of the chainsaw.

January 1952 brought *Flying Enterprise* and the end of the thirteen-day fight of Captain Kurt Carlsen and his companion, Ken Dancy, to keep the sinking freighter afloat and safely into Falmouth in what, with its newspaper, radio, film and television coverage, was probably the most public drama in the history of the sea. In the mid-afternoon, on Thursday 9 January, Carlsen and Dancy had to concede defeat as *Flying Enterprise* lay on her side, the funnel providing a gangway to the open sea and the rescue ships waiting a quarter of a mile away. My report, telephoned to news agencies in London, said that when it was obvious that the freighter's last minutes had come, Carlsen and Dancy pulled themselves out of

German submarine

the captain's cabin by the lifeline they had earlier prepared for a rapid escape. 'Then the two men, in a final act of heroism, climbed out along the funnel as the ship began to settle under them just forty-one miles off Falmouth. From its end they plunged into the sea and, five minutes later they were hauled to safety.

'It was an eerie sight in the deepening gloom. The water around her seemed to boil up with air pouring out of her hatches and ventilators. As if in tribute to the two heroes, some flares in the water began to ignite. Slowly she rose by the bows and seemed to stand in that position as if unwilling to accept her fate. Suddenly she plunged, stern first, and all that was left were bobbing debris — and a memory that will forever haunt those of us who saw it. Searchlights played on the scene and ships that had been bystanders in her death throes sounded their sirens in a last, sad mournful salute to *Flying Enterprise*.'

Fifteen years later it was shipwreck on an even greater and equally publicised scale as I covered the last moments of the oil

tanker *Torrey Canyon*, on the Seven Stones reef, between the Isles of Scilly and Land's End. On 18 March 1967, while carrying 117,000 tons of crude oil, she struck the reef at full speed, creating a threat of oil pollution on a scale never before experienced or even anticipated. After attempts to free her and remove her cargo had failed, and massive quantities of oil were coming ashore, the government decided, on 28 March, to bomb the ship in an attempt to break open the oil tanks and set fire to their contents.

From the safety of Land's End, I watched the area cleared of all aircraft and shipping, including the Seven Stones lightship. Buccaneer aircraft of the Royal Navy zoomed in on the wreck, dropping high explosive bombs to blow the covers off her oil tanks. A second wave of aircraft, this time Royal Air Force Hunters, flew over the gushing oil dropping 54,000 gallons of aviation fuel and sodium chlorate to prepare the scene for blitz by fire. A third wave then flew over *Torrey Canyon*, straffing the area with napalm.

At first there were only the sounds of muffled explosions. Then a spindly plume of black smoke drifted upwards, to be followed by the dense oily blackness that confirmed, to watchers on the shore, the success of the operation. According to the Royal Navy strike leader, Lieutenant Commander David Howard: 'The fire spread very quickly indeed, burning fiercely and giving off a lot of black smoke. On my next run I dropped two bombs on target. After the first four hits there was so much flame and smoke that it was difficult to see anything of the stern section at all. It got worse as we pumped more bombs into it. Smoke shot up to 8,000 feet and continued to rise rapidly. It got very black and dense and we had to alter the line of our attack to avoid firing through the smoke — and I was also rather worried in case the thing blew up.'

The morning of 1 August 1966 was one of those glorious summer days. As I drove towards Mylor, I was not unduly worried. I was on my way to a story that would, I felt sure, have a speedy and happy ending and would turn out to have been nothing more than a combination of misunderstanding and groundless fears. Such facts as were known were simple. A pleasure boat named *Darlwyne* had left Mylor the previous day on a round trip to Fowey. She had not returned to her moorings with her crew of two and her twenty-nine passengers. It seemed probable that, to avoid heavy weather, she

◀ The Author

had put in to a convenient cove for shelter and would, in due course, turn up none the worse.

I drove into the driveway of the house where the passengers had been staying. Although there was no sign of people, there was plenty of evidence that, but a few hours earlier, they had been alive and enjoying their holiday. From upstairs windows the inevitable display of bathing gear and towels fluttered with the merry signal of holiday gaiety. A car parked outside still had the confetti of a honeymoon couple. Makeshift cricket stumps, a tennis ball and a discarded sandal showed where children had, impatiently, had an impromptu game while waiting to be taken on the trip.

Everywhere the atmosphere was one of suspended life. At any moment, it seemed, the group — chattering excitedly of their night of unexpected drama — would walk down the drive asking for a hot breakfast and what the day's plans and pleasures were to be. Idly I waited, enjoying the peacefulness of the garden and wondering how I could make the story of an overdue pleasure boat sufficiently strong to warrant a mention on the mid-day news on a holiday weekend.

The story wrote itself, for already they were drowned, their bodies trapped inside *Darlwyne* in deep water off a hostile Cornish shore.

'SO BRAVE AND FAITHFUL A COMMANDER'

The month, October; the year, 1707. Sailing homeward from Toulon, in heavy seas, comes an English squadron of twenty-one ships, their sails straining as if to will them to the safety of their home port. In thick fog and gathering darkness, the fifteen ships of the line, the five fleet supply ships and the single yacht are well off course. They believe they are in deep water but, in reality, they are already committed to a course that will bring them among the murderous rocks to the west of the Isles of Scilly where the Atlantic Ocean meets the English Channel in a maelstrom of turbulence and ever-present death.

Then, through the stormy night comes the dull boom of a distress gun. Others join it in a muffled, mournful chorus. Surrounded by jagged rock, tossed by boiling seas, four of the squadron are already doomed as the seas around the Gilstone Ledges are filled with the first of what will be more than the bodies of 2,000 men in the grimmest disaster of the Royal Navy, and which will claim the life of admiral and able seaman, surgeon and ship's boy alike.

As the official records put it: '*Sir Cloudsley Shovel*, a Native of *Morson*, near *Clay*, in *Norfolk*, after arriving to high Honours in the Service of his Country, was lost near these Islands, upon the *Gilston Rock*, returning from *Thoulon*, October 22, 1707, and not upon the *Bishop* and *Clarks* as by some have been represented. It was thick foggy Weather, when the whole Fleet in Company coming (as they thought) near the Land, agreed to lye-to, in the Afternoon; but *Sir Cloudesly*, in the *Association*, ordering Sail to be made, first struck in the Night, and sunk immediately. Several Persons of Distinction being on board at that Time were lost; particularly the *Lady Shovel's* two Sons by her former Husband, *Sir John Narborough*, with about eight hundred Men. The *Eagle*, Capt. Hancock, Commander, underwent the same Fate. The *Rumney* and *Firebrand* also struck and were lost; but the two Captains and twenty-five of their Men were saved. The other Men of War in Company escaped by having timely Notice.'

What happened to cause so disastrous a loss? Almost certainly, a combination of error and miscalculation on the part of the fleet's navigators. Having entered the English Channel, they supposed themselves to be nearer the coast of France than the Isles of Scilly, and as the wind freshened from the south-south-west, they headed east by north in search of a mid-channel run home. They were, however, much further to the north than they had reckoned and on a converging course with the treacherous Western Rocks.

As *Association, Eagle, Romney* and *Firebrand* grounded, those aboard *Phoenix* were able to abandon ship before she, too, struck. *Royal Arms* was saved by the quick reaction of her Commander who, sensing rocks, changed course and scraped to safety. *St. George* followed *Association,* but the wave that carried the flagship onto the Gilstone floated the other ship away.

Scillonian legend has it that one man, a seaman from the Islands, recognised the position of the squadron, and dared to warn his officers of their peril. For this, the story goes, he was sentenced to be hanged. Offered a last request, he asked that the 109th Psalm be read aloud, with its curse: 'Let his days be few, and let another take his office. Let his children be fatherless, and his wife a widow ... Let his posterity be destroyed, and in the next generation let his name be clean put out. Because his mind was not to do good, but persecuted the poor, helpless man, that he might slay him that was vexed at heart.'

An official who visited Scilly in 1709, came up with a story that seemed to combine this legend with reality when he reported: 'After noon, Sir Cloudesley called a conference and examined masters what latitude they were in; all agreed to be in that of Ushant, on the coast of France, except Sir W. Jumper's master of the *Lenox,* who believed them to be nearer Scilly and that in three hours they should be in sight thereof. But Sir Cloudesley listened to not a single person whose opinion was contrary to the whole fleet.'

Perhaps there was no Scillonian seaman. Perhaps there was no hanging. Perhaps the 109th Psalm was not read. But the catastrophe took place.

It was a disaster in financial as well as human loss. The fleet was certainly carrying large quantities of money and valuable goods. On

14

Sir Cloudesley Shovel

the night before sailing from her last port homeward bound, *Association* was the setting for a lavish banquet for the Duke of Savoy. Sixty people who were entertained that night in the admiral's quarters dined off gold and silver plate so lavish that the Duke told Sir Cloudesley. 'Had you come to my palace at Turin, I could not have dined your excellency quite so well'. In addition, the Duke was able to borrow a large sum of money from the squadron's wages which were kept aboard *Association.*

A poem of the Scillies takes up the story:

> *Dark on Gilstone's rocky shore,*
> *The mist came lowering down;*
> *And night with all her deepening gloom,*
> *Put on her sable crown.*
> *How sad and awful was the sight,*
> *How black and dark the shore.*
> *Two thousand souls went down that night,*
> *And ne'er saw daylight more.*

The narrative continues through the official report: 'At the East Part of *St. Mary's Island* in *Porth-hellic* Bay, the Body of *Sir Cloudesley* came a-shore by the Tide, after floating past several Rocks and lesser Islands. Some relate he was first found upon a Hatch, with a Little Dog dead by him, he endeavouring, by that Means, to save himself. He is said to be taken up by a Soldier belonging to *St. Mary's* Garrison, who buried him in the Sand at *Porth-hellic.* Being afterwards sought, he was discovered by the Marks on his Body, where he had been wounded, and was removed from thence by the Purser of the *Arundel* on Board that Ship in the Harbour, where he was embalmed by the Order of the Commander. His Body was thence conveyed to *Plymouth* by the *Salisbury,* lying in State there in the Citadel, till Lady Shovel ordered the Removal of it to her House in *Soho-Square, London.'*

Although much of the story has been filled in by the guesswork of generations of Scillonian story-tellers, bits of it are well documented. Mr Herbert, Deputy Paymaster-General of Marine Regiments, for instance, was with the body from its exhumation at Porthellick until it was handed over to the pathologist, Dr James Yonge, at Plymouth's Royal Citadel.

'I was by the grave when he was lifted,' he recorded. 'His ring was lost from off his hand . . . Sir Cloudesley had on him a pair of thread

Sir Cloudesley's 'grave' on St Mary's

stockings and a thread waistcoat . . . we knew him to be Sir Cloudesley by a certain black mole under his left ear, as also by the first joint of one of his forefingers being broken inwards formerly by playing at tables; the said joint of his finger was also small and tapered, as well as standing somewhat inwards; he had likewise a shot in his right arm, another in his left thigh. Moreover we were well satisfied that it was he, for he was as fresh when his face was washed as if only asleep; his nose likewise bled as though alive . . . Many that saw him said his head was the largest that they had seen, and not at all swelled with the water, neither had he any bruise or scar about him, save only a small scratch above one of his eyes, like that of a pin. He was a very lusty, comely man, and very fat.'

Mr Herbert duly delivered the corpse to Dr Yonge, who reported: 'The corpse of Sir Cloudesley Shovel was brought into the Citadel. He had been unfortunately drowned nine days, and I embalmed him and had £50 for it. The corpse was carried to London and buried in Westminster Abbey at the Queen's cost.'

17

Sir Cloudesley's tomb in Westminster Abbey

18

Such recognition was an outstanding tribute to his prowess as a seaman and leader at a time when those who failed their men and nation were dismissed in disgrace, if not actually court-martialled and executed. His funeral was, therefore, complete absolution from any responsibility for the loss of 2,000 men that England could ill-afford.

On 23 December 1707, his body was carried from his home, in Soho Square, to a waiting gun-carriage pulled by dozens of sailors on the two-mile journey to Westminster Abbey through crowded and silent streets. 'The body was buried with all pomp and magnificence suitable to Her Majesty's high regard to the remains of so brave and faithful a commander. There were at the ceremony the Queen's trumpets, kettle drums, and household drums with other music; The Queen's and the Prince's watermen in their liveries, most of the nobility's coaches with six horses, the flag-officers that were in town, and the Prince's Council, the Heraldsmen-at-Arms, and the Knights' Marshal men.

'His body was reposited in Westminster Abbey among the heroes of renown, where the sad memorable story is written upon his tombstone.'

3-ton gun recovered from the wreck of *HMS Association*

'AN OUTRAGEOUS TEMPEST OF THE SEA'

For more than two thousand years, seamen have known of Falmouth as a harbour of refuge where they could lie in safety while wild seas lashed the Cornish coastline or, if victim of storm or hurricane, they could shelter and have the ravages of the elements put right before venturing, once more, onto the High Seas.

On 14 January 1814, however, there was played out in the safety of this great harbour a drama recalled by a memorial tablet to 136 people laid in a mass grave in Mylor churchyard: 'To the memory of the warriors, women and children who, returning from the coast of Spain, unhappily perished in the wreck of the *Queen*, transport, on Trefusis Point, January 14th, 1814. This stone is erected as a testimony of regret by the inhabitants of this parish.'

Just before Christmas 1813, *Queen* had sailed from Lisbon bringing home men and their families from Lord Wellington's army in the Peninsular war. Included in their number were some who were wounded or sick, together with several French prisoners of war.

Although bound for Portsmouth, *Queen* put into Falmouth for shelter and to replenish her stores for the last leg of the journey home. On 10 January a storm blew up, and the master — Captain Carr — laid out an extra anchor as a safety measure. For three days it held. Then, on the Thursday afternoon, it began to drag. For some strange reason the slight drift of the transport was not noticed for some time by those on board. Too late they realised their danger. As they rushed to get another anchor out, the existing one broke away as its cable parted.

As *Queen* drifted towards the rocks of Trefusis, panic reigned

Memorial in Mylor Churchyard to those drowned in the wreck of the *Queen*▶

20

To the
Memory of the
WARRIORS,
Women and Children,
who on their return to England
from the Coast of Spain;
unhappily perished
in the Wreck of the
Queen Transport,
on Trefusis Point, Jan.y 14, 1814

This Stone is erected as a Testimony
of regret for their fate, by the
Inhabitants of this Parish.

Mylor Churchyard

aboard. Soldiers and civilians got in the way of the crew. When the distress cannon was primed, the sea soaked the powder and the gun was useless. Falling snow hid the ship from the shore as she drove towards disaster.

She struck. Captain Carr ordered the masts to be cut away, but as he did so, the ship was hit by a succession of heavy waves that ground her further onto the rocks. Guns broke from their mountings and trundled to and fro, running down those who were unable to jump aside. Within twenty minutes many of those on board were either crushed to death or drowned, leaving but ninety-eight survivors of the 348 living souls who had been so eagerly looking forward to their homes but a short while before.

The West Briton reported: 'She parted her cable and went ashore at Trefusis Point, where she became a complete wreck in twenty minutes after she struck. At this awful moment there were upwards of 330 persons on board. The horror and confusion that ensued is

22

indescribable; those who got on deck were either swept off by the waves or maimed by the fragments of the rigging and spars that flew about in all directions. Numbers could not make their way up, and as the vessel's bottom was speedily beaten to pieces, they were drowned or crushed to death by the floating pieces.

'The return of day presented a shocking spectacle. Dead bodies of men, women and children, many of them mangled, several of them naked and others scarcely half-dressed, strewed the shore.'

Three years earlier Falmouth had recoiled to another shipping horror when in a gale the 36-gun frigate *HMS Franchise* collided with the transport *Jane* with the loss of 269 lives.

Across Falmouth bay, on the dreaded Manacles, a further 280 died in a night of terror when the transport *Dispatch*, and the brig *HMS Primrose* came to grief in January 1809 on the way back from Corunna with a unit of the 7th Dragoons. *Dispatch*, which had run the gauntlet of enemy gunfire on her voyage home, went down leaving only seven survivors whilst, from *Primrose*, only a young lad reached safety.

Gun from *HMS Primrose*

HMS Primrose **memorial**

Almost three hundred years earlier another famous ship had been wrecked on the Lizard coast. She was *St Andrew*, owned by King John III of Portugal, and carrying treasure said to be worth £16,000. Driven by 'an outrageous tempest of the sea', she was thrown, on 19 January 1526 onto the coast near Gunwalloe. Local residents rallied to the rescue of many of the crew . . . and then turned their muscles to salvaging the ship's treasure of silver, gold and jewellery, as well as fine silks and tapestries. They buried these in the sand dunes near the church.

Their action of recovery was misunderstood and local magistrates were promptly ordered to locate and hand over the 'salvaged' goods to representatives of King Henry VIII at the request of King John. This posed quite a problem for the trio of local worthies as they had organised the looting. In court at Helston they entered the outrageous plea that their behaviour was 'the custom of the county', adding that the man in charge of the cargo had begged them to take the spoils into their custody 'fearing lest the country people might carry

Gunwalloe Church and rocks

them off into their homes where they be lost forever'. They had, they admitted, retained a little of their 'good work' in order to provide food, clothing, warmth and comfort for the survivors of the shipwreck.

In November 1720, 704 men drowned — and only three lived — when the transport *Royal Anne*, outward bound for Barbados, went down after hitting a rock off the Lizard. For days afterwards, bodies washed ashore like pieces of seaweed after a storm. They were mostly buried in mass graves in nearby Pistol Meadow. Each body, of soldier, sailor, civilian or child alike, had to be carried from the seashore to the mass graves in a gruesome task that took several days. Horror increased as packs of dogs attacked the corpses before they could be covered with earth. For generations afterwards, it was said, the people of the Lizard were so ashamed of the way that dogs had violated the dead that they were banished, even from farms.

When the famous novelist, Wilkie Collins, visited the Lizard in the mid-1800s, he noted the absence of dogs. This, he said, con-

The *Olympe* ashore at Gunwalloe, 1910

firmed that the story was one of fact rather than of legend.

Porthleven recorded a serious shipwreck in December 1814 when the salt-carrier *Atalanta* was lost with her crew of five after running aground, and also claimed the lives of three would-be rescuers. Reporting the loss, *The Royal Cornwall Gazette* expressed concern over the fact that 'The sea, running very high, none of the cargo could be saved and the vessel, once driven ashore, went to pieces soon after. Six bodies have since been found, on which a coroner's inquest has been held. It is to be regretted that the crew were unacquainted with the new harbour at Porthleven as they might have run in there, even in its present unfinished state, and lain in perfect safety.'

Drink and the general disinterest of the master were factors raised at the official inquiry into the sinking of the emigrant ship *John* on the Manacles on 3 May 1855. Only hours earlier, with 263 people on board seeking a new life in Canada, she had sailed from Plymouth amidst scenes of farewell and celebration. Accommodated aboard were 149 adults, ninety-eight children, sixteen babies and a crew of sixteen. Her master was Captain Edward Rawle.

In good weather she sailed down the Cornish coast, arriving off Falmouth at about 9.30 in the evening. After passing St Anthony, one of the officers was worried that he had not picked up the Lizard light. He called Captain Rawle who, after a brief look at the weather, dismissed the view of the mate that *John* was too close to the land for safety, and went to bed.

Within a matter of moments the ship hit the Manacles and rode over the top of the outer reefs before coming to an abrupt halt on Lowland Point. For some strange reason the master and his crew did not seem at all concerned about the plight of their ship and its passengers. Instead, after breaking open the ship's liquor supplies, they sat in the rigging well above the water and calmly drank themselves into oblivion.

Benjamin Skewes, a shoemaker from Falmouth, was a witness at the investigation held two weeks later. He did not see the captain, mates or crew help the passengers in any way, he said. He thought that Captain Rawle had been drinking; he was smelling of liquor but he could not swear that the officer was drunk.

The inquiry was told a harrowing narrative. As the crew looked down from their lofty perch, they actually beat off passengers

27

trying to join them. As waves crashed across the deck, passengers were swilled over the side and into the black waters. Those who were clinging to ropes lost their grip in the bitter cold and disappeared forever. When rescue boats arrived from Coverack and Porthoustock, the crew became animated and fought for places irrespective of the needs of their passengers. Although there were seventy survivors, not a single crew member lost his life. And, the inquiry heard, they even took all their possessions ashore with them.

John, it was found, carried no signal gun or distress flares or rockets. Her dinghies were not in a seaworthy condition. Captain Rawle was charged with manslaughter, and sent to prison. The entire crew, with the exception of one steward who showed great courage, were publicly censured for their cowardly, selfish and inhuman behaviour.

Another loss inquiry, four years later, complimented the bravery and dedication of Lizard coastguards and volunteer helpers for putting out on a treacherous coast in ordinary boats to go to the rescue of those aboard the stricken steamer *Czar*, which grounded after hugging the cliffs in an attempt to gain shelter from a gale. She was loaded with guns, ammunition, stores and uniforms for the British garrison in Malta.

She hit Vrogue Rock with such an impact that she split in two, the two portions sinking as they drifted apart. Her skipper, Captain Robert Jackson, thought first of the safety of his crew, although his wife and young son were aboard. He ordered nine or ten non-swimmers into the larger of the ship's boats, but they were drowned when it capsized. Another boat got safely away, and other swimmers were picked up by volunteers from the shore.

It was then that Captain Jackson looked for his wife and child. He discovered that they were trapped in a cabin that was already under water. He was still trying to rescue them when the section of the ship sank and he went down while still fighting, unsuccessfully, to free them.

On 10 March 1873 *The West Briton* told its readers: 'Five of the drowned sailors who belong to the *Boyne*, of Scarborough, wrecked at Mullion on Saturday last, have been washed ashore more or less mutilated. A thigh and a hand have also been picked up. A sailor who survived stated that as the ship broke up he noticed one of his ship-mates nearly cut in two.'

28

Left: memorial to those drowned in the emigrant ship *John.*

Below: wreck of the *Suffolk* on the Lizard in 1886. 100 of the 163 cows on board were lost, but the 45 people reached safety.

In thick weather, *Boyne* was way off course. Instead of entering Falmouth bay, she was heading towards vertical cliffs. She hit them, and literally bounced back, broadside on, to the waves. The crew fired distress flares but, due to the height of the cliffs and the angle, they did little more than show — briefly — at cliff-top level before falling back into the sea. Eventually they were spotted by a farmer who ran to Mullion to alert the lifeboat.

In the meantime the Coastguard had arrived on the cliff-top, but found that *Boyne* had already broken in half and that, in a very heavy swell, the crew were fighting a grim battle to hold onto the ship's rails although obviously exhausted. So exhausted, in fact, and in such a state of shock that they could not grab the lifeline as it was fired to them. One by one, as the rescuers watched, the sea plucked the seamen from their precarious hold until all fifteen had been swept to their deaths. Even the lifeboat could not help.

There were, however, four survivors. Just after *Boyne* hit the cliffs, an apprentice and three men launched the barque's skiff. Lying as close as they dared, they called on their colleagues to join them. The captain ordered them to row away, his last words being 'Good luck to you'. When taken aboard the Mullion lifeboat, they were found to be more dead than alive. But, unlike their fifteen colleagues, they lived to sail again.

The month of March 1891 brought its share of death and disaster to Cornwall's southern coast. First came the loss, with all hands, of the small sailing ships *Edwin* and *Aquilon,* off Porthoustock in weather so bad that the local lifeboat could not be launched and her crew climbed to the foot of the cliffs to see if they could, using ropes, cheat the sea of its toll.

Next day came the report that a large sailing ship was being driven onto rocks under the cliffs at Porthallow bay. As would-be rescuers rushed through the wind and heavy showers of sleet and snow, they saw a four-masted ship, fully rigged, aground and with waves throwing themselves over her. Sailing from Calcutta with jute for Dundee, *Bay of Panama* had grounded with such force that she had shattered one mast, and lost her fore and main topmasts. Even as she grounded, a freak wave engulfed her and swamped the cabin, drawing the captain, his wife, their steward and four apprentices over the side and to their deaths as it eddied back.

Taking command, the mate ordered everyone to climb out of the sea's reach up the rigging. The carpenter and sail maker, seeking

Bay of Panama

shelter behind the wheelhouse, were sought out by the probing billows, and dragged into the oblivion of death. The bosun reached a safe perch on the rigging, but suffered a brain storm and jumped into the sea and was never seen, alive, again. Six other men, in soaking clothing, froze to death. Others, overcome with exhaustion, fell among the merciless waves.

A breeches-buoy was sent out to the ship but, by then, there were only seventeen men left to rescue out of a ship's company of forty. Even then their ordeal was not over. Having rested, bathed and been fed at St Keverne, the pathetic group set off for Falmouth in the local horse-drawn 'bus. Nature was still against them and they found that, with snow drifts blocking their way, they had seemingly only exchanged death by drowning for death from exposure. But the men of *Bay of Panama*, having cheated fate once, were determined to beat it again. They struggled, on foot, to Falmouth, enduring, as *The Falmouth Packet* put it, 'as much privation in that walk as they did in the actual shipwreck'.

The liner *Suevic* stranded on the Maenheere Rocks

If the Lizard claimed ships, it did not always seek lives as well. Compared with stories of confusion, bad seamanship and disregard for the lives of others, that of the White Star Company's liner *Suevic*, stranded on the Maenheere Rocks, near the Lizard on 17 March 1907, is an outstanding one of discipline and organisation. In drizzle and generally bad weather, she was homeward bound from Australia and due to make an intermediate call at Plymouth before docking in London. There were 382 passengers on board, 141 crew members — and a stowaway.

At 10.25 p.m., an officer spotted the Lizard lighthouse almost overhead, synchronised with the look-out's cry: 'breakers ahead'. Desperately the officer of the watch tried to swing the ship to seaward, but it was to no avail and she ran onto the rocks at full speed.

What happened then was an almost copybook example of abandoning ship. As distress signals flashed out by rocket, flare and lamp, passengers were escorted to their assembly points while boat crews prepared the lifeboats. Officers reassured the passengers that there was no cause for alarm and that lifeboats were already on their way from the Lizard and Cadgwith and would soon be alongside. In addition, the lifeboats from Coverack and Porthleven had been launched and a tug was coming from Falmouth.

In complete calm, the survivors took to the liner's lifeboats and rowed towards the approaching rescue craft. Cadgwith lifeboat had on board the local lifeboat secretary, the Reverend Henry Vyvyan, and he took command of one of the ship's lifeboats and led it to safety to free the Cadgwith boat to resume its task. With lifeboats ferrying survivors, tugs acting as tenders, and the ship's lifeboats being towed, the complete and safe evacuation of *Suevic* was completed well within twelve hours from the grounding to the landing of the last survivor.

The outstanding nature of the rescue was recognised by the award of six silver medals by the Royal National Lifeboat Institution. In addition to one to the Reverend Vyvyan, the Institution also recognised two crew members of *Suevic*, George Anderson and William Williams, for their exemplary skill, care and conduct in carrying children and the sick down rope ladders and dropping them safely into the arms of lifeboatmen despite the complications of a heavy swell.

'THE USUAL CEREMONY, FOR AN OFFICER OF HIS RANK, WAS OBSERVED'

Within an hour of being rescued, Second Lieutenant Thomas Gill of His Majesty's Ship *Anson* sat down in an office in Helston, on 29 December 1807. With great thought, he wrote to the Secretary to the Lords Commissioners of the Admiralty.

'I am truly sorry it devolves on me to acquaint you for the information of their Lordships of the loss of His Majesty's Ship *Anson* — She was wrecked this morning near Port Leven about two miles from this place. The Captain and First Lieut. were both drowned and the ship without doubt will be a total loss. As nearly as I can find out about 140 of the Officers and Crew were saved. She sailed from Falmouth on the 24. inst. for our Station off the Black Rocks. The next day it came on to blow and continued increasing till the morning of the 28th; when the Captain thought proper to bear up for Falmouth; the same night about four o'clock we made land to the Westward of the Lizard and in a situation that compelled us to anchor. At 4 the next morning we parted the best bower, and at 7 the small bower, when the Captain directed the ship to run on shore.

Twenty four hours later another letter was on its way to the Admiralty, this time from the Customs House, Penzance, and added these details: 'Captain Lydiard and Mr. Ferris the First Lieutenant are amongst those who have met a watery grave. The number of lives that are supposed to be lost in this melancholy affair amount to about 50, but in this statement I may not be correct . . . . The Beach is covered with wreck, and I am apprehensive there will be little of her Stores salved.'

Charles Lydiard, Captain, Royal Navy, had an outstanding record in the Service. He was regarded as a resourceful officer possessing cool and determined bravery, and — in the year of the loss of *HMS Anson* — featured in glowing reports praising his seamanship as well as his leadership. He was buried in Falmouth with 'the usual

HMS Anson **was run aground on Loe Bar in 1807**

ceremony for an Officer of Captain Lydiard's rank being observed upon the occasion', on 2 January 1808. Yet, three days later, a Court Martial held in Plymouth and presided over by two Rear Admirals and eleven fellow Captains was convened to investigate the loss of the twenty-six year old frigate and the conduct of her commander.

Returning to the shelter of Falmouth, *Anson* was caught by a combination of wind and tide and driven towards the shore. To lessen her motion, Lydiard ordered the top gallant masts to be lowered to deck and the largest anchors to be put out. Early next morning, as Gill had told the Lords Commissioners, the largest anchor parted, followed three hours later, by the smaller.

Lydiard, despite his affection for the ship in which he had served for several years, decided that the lives of his men had to be his prime concern and gave orders for *Anson* to be run on the long shingle ridge outside Porthleven, Loe Bar. He entrusted his Master, Hugh Steward, to carry out the operation in the safest possible way. Steward, later found by the Court Martial to have failed to carry out, in every respect, the duties and responsibilities of his position, may have misjudged the tricky operation with the result that *Anson* hit

Loe Bar today

the ridge and turned on her side, still some way off the safety of the beach. Between ship and land there was a wide area of stormy sea, with a combination of wind and dropping tide dragging survivors and wreckage seawards instead of inshore. The only link with the shore was a terrifying catwalk created by the mainmast, and often obscured by breaking waves and clouds of spray.

The Customs officer at Penzance was wildly wrong in his belief that fifty men had been lost. The final tally was nearer 110, as seaman after seaman was either washed away by the breakers, or crushed or injured by falling spars.

The coast was thronged by the usual band of sightseers who, as so often in times of shipping disaster, could watch and listen — but could not help as the wreck was out of reach. They could see and hear Captain Lydiard coolly restoring confidence, discipline and control among his men. One by one he encouraged those aboard to make the monkey-run to safety, not letting them falter if the man in front stumbled into the sea and was washed away.

Captain Charles Lydiard, RN

Eventually it was his turn to run the gauntlet. As he prepared himself for the dangerous dash, he spotted a young seaman who was literally frozen to the wreck less fearful to stay than he was to try to escape. In a few sentences he reassured the youngster and asked him to make a joint effort. With one arm locked, reassuringly, around the boy, and with the other seeking the firmness of the rigging, he edged them both onto the narrow, slippery, rounded mast. Half way across, he slipped. In his exhaustion he could not recover or hold on. Captain and young seaman died together.

As the Court Martial put it to Steward: 'How was his death occasioned?' The response: 'He quit the ship about threequarters of an hour after she struck. He was then much exhausted. By his perserverance in remaining so long by the wreck, his strength was at length so exhausted that he could not get through the surf.'

Lydiard's heroic death acted as a spur to the conscience and the courage of those on the beach. Men threw themselves into the surf in an attempt to swim out to the wreck. Time after time the sea threw them back, until exhausted, they accepted the despair and disappointment of defeat. One burly farmer, a Mr Roberts, was a strong swimmer. Tying a rope around his waist, he hurled himself into the sea and, after a desperate battle, reached *Anson*. The rope was quickly secured and provided another route to safety.

As the tide continued to drop, other would-be rescuers waded up to their arm pits, edging forward a few inches at a time as the gap between themselves and the frigate narrowed to something approaching swimming range. One of them, a Methodist lay preacher from Mullion, Mr William Foxwell, was determined to get aboard in case there were any men trapped in the disintegrating hull. Urging others to follow him, he reached the ship and found several people lying below, either too exhausted or too paralysed with fear to move. Some, he said later, 'in terror and despair, called upon God for mercy; others, in a more hopeful trust, seemed resigned to their fate; and others were so weak as to be indifferent to the horrors around them.' Together with other rescuers, he coaxed the survivors to safety.

Some time later both Mr Foxwell and Mr Roberts each received a silver medal. On one side was an engraving of the shipwreck scene,

◀ The *Anson* memorial above Loe Bar

and on the other the words: 'One of the humble Instruments under Divine Providence of saving the Lives of Fellow Creatures Wreck'd in the *Anson* Frigate on the Loe Bar — 29 December 1807. This medal is given by his Country'.

As the bodies of the dead were gradually returned by the sea, they were buried in a huge, unmarked, grave. No burial prayers were said for fear that, amongst those who had perished, there might be non-Christians. Other corpses were laid in local churchyards, including those of Midshipman Richard Leech, aged eleven years; and of Robert Smith, Surgeon of *Anson* and his own son, who found a final resting place at St Michael's Church, Helston.

After two more days, the only activity at Loe Bar was that of patrols of Excisemen and soldiers collecting up, and taking into protective custody, such uncontaminated stores and casks of rum and other valuable items as escaped from the submerged wreck which, even then, was settling deep into the restless sands in front of Loe Bar.

On 5 January 1808, the Court Martial opened aboard *HMS Salvador del Mundo*, in Plymouth. Due to the death of Captain Lydiard and the First Lieutenant, it was the unfortunate Second Lieutenant, Thomas Gill, who found himself on trial. Naval tradition demanded that the senior officer surviving the loss of any ship should be answerable, and the Court was convened: 'to try Lieutenant Thomas Gill and other surviving Officers and ship's Company of His Majesty's late Ship *Anson* for their conduct upon the occasion of her running on shore, and loss, on the 29 December last, at Port Leven near Helston, in Cornwall'.

Finding that *Anson* 'was not prepared in a state of readiness to come to an anchor upon a lee shore in such tremendous weather as the Ship had to encounter', the Court Martial admonished the Master, Hugh Steward. Other than in the case of Steward, the Court was of the opinion that 'no blame be attached to any of the surviving Officers or Ship's Company'.

'... A THOUSAND FRAGMENTS STREWED MOUNT'S BAY'

In simple, but movingly eloquent terms, *The Royal Cornwall Gazette* told the story, in February 1872, of the loss of the barque *Manitobah*, on the Bucks rocks, in Mount's Bay.

'There were on board Captain Durkee, his wife and two children, two mates and ten seamen. About midnight on Wednesday, with a heavy southerly gale, and two lights sighted at intervals, she was running away, as it was thought, for the Bristol Channel. It was very thick and dark and altogether a bad night at sea, and the wind had veered rather to the east of south. All seemed well, however, until the alarm of "land" and "breakers" was raised. The only chance was to wear ship, and this was tried; but she struck violently on the westernmost Buck, was soon washed off again, and in a few minutes was driven on shore. Then came the old story of huge seas breaking over the vessel and no hope. The captain, with the elder of his two children — a little one of three years, — in his arms, dropped onto a rock and endeavoured to reach shore, but was quickly swept away, and lost his child. But stunned, bruised and half-drowned, he at last reached the cliffs, scrambled up them with the object of getting to the depot of a rocket apparatus, or procuring assistance (for his wife and an infant of fifteen months were aboard) but wandered about the, to him, unknown cliffs and fields until, in an hour, he found a farmhouse and aroused the inmates. In the meantime the vessel was fast going to pieces. A tremendous sea swept away the wife and the child with the pilot house in which they had taken refuge. One seaman also perished.

'At daylight scarcely any of the vessel was to be seen inside the Bucks, but a thousand fragments strewed Mount's Bay.'

Captain Durkee, with tragic consequences for all but himself, had mistaken the Wolf lighthouse for that on St Agnes, having failed — in the storm — to notice the distinctive red flash of the Wolf.

Throughout the long history of shipwreck around Land's End, the conduct, sobriety, or seamanship of the master of the lost vessel has often been called into question at the subsequent inquest or inquiry. In 1867, for instance, it was claimed that there would have been more survivors from *John Gray*, aground at Long Rock, near Penzance, had not the master threatened to shoot any of his men who took advantage of a lifeline fired on board by the coast rescue team. The line was not used, and six men died — despite the superhuman efforts of Penzance lifeboatmen both in reaching the wreck and in persuading at least thirteen men to jump to safety.

Then there was *Oriental*, lost with all hands off Lamorna, in October of the same year, after her cargo of timber shifted and caused her to capsize whilst on the last leg of her voyage from Quebec to Liverpool. Ironically, although the ship became a total wreck, and fifteen men died, the timber was salvaged and later sold at a good price.

In May 1868 another ship hit the Bucks. This time it was the iron steamer *Garonne*, of Liverpool. Once more faulty navigation was involved. With a general cargo, an experienced crew, and a complement of sixteen passengers including eight children, *Garonne* was no stranger to the area. She sailed a regular schedule between Liverpool and Bordeaux, and had a Cornishman, Benjamin Drew, as her master. His regular course took him close to the Longships lighthouse and across Land's End into the Bristol Channel. At lunchtime on 22 May, he brought his ship onto her usual course, but was unable — in poor visibility — to spot either the Longships or the Wolf. This didn't concern him unduly, but he became worried when the patent log — on which proof of calculations depended — was found to be non-operational. Working on his estimates of the distance covered since he had last been able to confirm his position, Drew put on extra speed to clear the area. Hardly had he done so than he received the call 'Land ahead'. Automatically he ordered the wheel to be put to hard a-starboard, and the engines to full astern.

He was too late. With an ominous crunch, the vessel hit the Bucks, took water, and began to sink. Rockets were fired and distress flares were burned, but these were not understood by the two schooners that were in the vicinity. Drew ordered the boats to be swung out, but found that those on the starboard side were hanging over the rocks to which *Garonne* seemed welded. To shelter the passengers while the boats on the other side were made ready, Drew told them to wait in the shelter of the poop — only to see some of them washed

Mill Bay, Land's End, 1832

overboard by the clutching waves.

As the ship's dinghy reached the sea, it was discovered that it was loaded with green peas — which Drew had been carrying as part of a little private trading — and that the bung was missing. Using a piece of wood, the ship's carpenter made a makeshift plug and the dinghy was pronounced seaworthy.

By this time, Captain Drew was beyond taking an active role in the attempt to abandon ship. Instead of leading the operation, he wandered the deck of *Garonne* muttering 'Lord have mercy on us'. Of twenty-two crew members, four were already drowned. All but two of the passengers — a father and son — were dead. Tragically, even the father was not to live for, although rescued, he was so overtaken with grief at the loss of his wife and three other of his children, that he died of exposure and sorrow soon after reaching the safety of Mousehole.

As a newspaper report put it: 'Cornwall can tell many a saga of disaster at sea; but this tale of the little *Garonne*, transfixed on the

The Seven Stones lightship today

Bucks, the group of terrified women and children being ruthlessly snatched from her stern by the leaping waves, and the captain, in classical tradition, electing to go down with his ship, is surely the most heart-rending of them all.'

Another mistake was probably responsible for the tragedy that overwhelmed the Government lighter, *Devon*, off Lamorna, in October 1868, when the look-out incorrectly thought that the Brisons rocks were two ships riding at anchor without lights.

In the twenty minutes between the false identification and the complete destruction of *Devon*, seventeen of the eighteen people on board were drowned. The only survivor, a man named Davis, avoided death because he jumped into the sea on the seaward side of the wreck, and escaped being caught in the suction between ship and rocks which either drowned his colleagues or crushed or pulverised them in a matter of moments. Sharing death with the captain and his crew were a woman passenger and her two children, who were accompanying their father, a young Royal Marine.

Equally short-lived was the disaster that overtook the Italian barque *Luigina Reanchette*, near Lamorna, on 23 November 1872. In heavy weather, she hit the Bucks and sank almost immediately with the loss of her entire crew, the first sign of the tragedy being when folk at Lamorna wondered why there were casks of tallow coming ashore amongst other pieces of wreckage, and why the crane on the harbourside, and the neighbouring cliffs, were festooned with strands of wool.

A search of the coast revealed eight bodies and evidence of the loss of the ship.

Another unwitnessed loss was that of the Glasgow-registered sailing ship *Barremann*, on Pollard Rock, near the Seven Stones reef, in July 1887. The first suspicion of a tragedy arose when a local fishing boat reported having sighted the topmast of a vessel sticking out of the water. Because of bad weather conditions, she had not investigated.

Within three days the mast had vanished, but pieces of wreckage — as well as a ship's name board carrying the inscription *Barremann* — had appeared on local beaches. When the crew of the Seven Stones lightship were relieved, they said that, on 6 July, they had glimpsed what seemed to be a large sailing ship near Pollard Rock, and apparently aground. Because of bad weather they had not been able to carry out a search, but had later spotted debris floating past their vessel. It was only when the records of overdue ships were checked that it was possible to confirm that *Barremann*, loaded with cement, pig-iron and coal, was missing — presumed lost — with twenty-seven men drowned.

It was a case of lost, presumed drowned, too in the wreck of the Austrian barque *Fratelli Fabris*, on the Runnelstone, on 21 February 1892. Early that day, watchers at Lamorna saw a small boat containing five men being rowed towards the shore. Suddenly a huge wave capsized the tiny craft and the men disappeared into the heaving seas. None were seen alive again, although the empty punt carried the name of the barque which was recorded as having hit the rock and sunk in deep water.

On a January morning in 1937, the Belgian trawler *Vierge Marie* came to grief on the cliffs near Sennen. Suffering from engine trouble, she was limping along the coast towards Newlyn and those on board were unaware of how the distance had narrowed between themselves and the steep cliffs until she grounded.

Although she put out a distress call, it was necessary to abandon ship before help could arrive. In the process the cabin boy, Valentine Maartens, was lost overboard. The master, Josef Lus; the mate, Gustave Vanlee; the chief engineer, and two seamen, took to the dinghy which then capsized. Lus and Vanlee started to swim ashore, but the other men righted the small boat and started to row away from the threatening and towering cliffs. Seeing the searchlight of Penlee lifeboat, they pulled towards it — only to capsize once more. They were pulled to safety, but died before they could be landed at Newlyn. Meanwhile, Lus and Vanlee survived a nightmare swim amongst jagged rocks and then climbed the cliffs before finding safety in a neighbouring cottage.

In November 1948, eleven men died — and one lived — after the French ship *Saint Guenole* went aground at Gribba Head, and capsized.

Following the interception of a distress call, in March 1956, Penlee lifeboat put to sea. All that was known was that an unidentified ship, referring to itself as 'Dieppe 1517' was in difficulties. 'Dieppe 1517' was soon established as the registration of the motor trawler *Vert Prairial*, and which could be anywhere between Brixham and the fishing grounds off Padstow. At first light, the authorities were telephoned with a report of a large trawler aground near Porthcurno. As the lifeboat approached the wreck it passed several bodies floating nearby. Two were recovered, and the rest were left to drift ashore.

There were no survivors. Seventeen men had died in the tragedy and there was no clue as to why she had run aground and as to whether the distress call had been sent out as a consequence of engine failure or, perhaps, when her crew realised that shipwreck was imminent on the hostile shore.

A few days later the bodies of most of the crew were loaded aboard another fishing vessel, *Gai Floreal*, to be returned to their home port for burial. Seamen have a superstition about carrying bodies and, perhaps, it came as little surprise when, in 1962, *Gai Floreal* was involved in what seemed to be an action replay of the loss of *Vert Prairial*, becoming fixed to rocks under the cliffs near Zennor. On this occasion, however, a combination of rescue services achieved what was described as 'a chance in a million' mission in saving the whole crew and helping release the trawler from her jagged bed.

The coaster *Juan Ferrer* lost in October 1963 ▶

Spanish seamen, too, have died in the waters off Lamorna. Few, perhaps, more terribly than the eleven of the crew of fifteen of the coaster *Juan Ferrer* which was lost with horrific suddenness in October 1963. Once more it was a case of taking liberties with an unfamiliar and unfriendly shore. In the early hours of the morning the distress frequencies carried one short, urgent call: 'Aground in the vicinity of Land's End. Before the identification could be completed or repeated, *Juan Ferrer* had capsized. Water flooded her electrical system and she was left without any lights or any way of guiding rescuers to her presumed position.

With nothing to go on, rescue units assembled at Land's End and started an intensive search designed to cover ten miles of coastline. After several hours they spotted a man in the sea clinging to wreckage. He was the coaster's master, and he had stayed on board until his ship sank before committing himself to four hours in the sea without a lifejacket until being picked up by the Penzance lifeboat. As the Coastguard and their helpers combed the cliffs and shoreline, they found three other men walking, safely, towards them having rested on the rocks before climbing the cliffs.

One of the most incredible wreck and rescue stories of Land's End involved the French trawler *Jeanne Gougy*. Homeward-bound for Dieppe from the Irish fishing grounds, she seemed to be making — in November 1962 — for the red sector of the Longships light. Coastguards tried to follow her progress, but lost sight of her in the sudden squalls of rain and heavy seas. At 5 a.m., distress flares soared into the sky. *Jeanne Gougy* was firmly aground at Land's End, and being battered to pieces.

In charge of the Coastguard was Divisional Officer William Bridger, who later recalled: 'As we went to the scene of the wreck we could hear the terrible crunching of a ship being broken to pieces by the tide, the seas and the rocks. We could hear, too, the terrified screams of the men on board as their ship broke up beneath them and the seas broke over the wheelhouse.'

Rescue units were joined by life-saving teams from St Just and Sennen, together with Sennen Cove lifeboat.

Mr Bridger went on: 'We fired parachute flares and in their light we could see the terrible scene below. We fired half a dozen rocket

◀ French trawler *Jeanne Gougy* aground at Land's End

lines across her and three of them actually fell within reach of the men within the wheelhouse. Four men tried to get the lines, but the sea broke over them and we never saw them alive again.' Everyone except Mr Bridger gave up hope of saving anyone from the wreck. He refused to give up the fight, and called for an RAF helicopter, convinced that there could be other men sheltering in some compartment. Although well into his sixties, he said that he would try to board the wreck as soon as the tide ebbed.

Towards noon, a woman on the cliffs said that she was sure she had seen something move in the wheelhouse. As the rescue party looked, they saw an arm come through the wheelhouse window and heard a voice calling out in French. They shouted to the man to stay where he was, but lost sight of him as another huge wave engulfed the wheelhouse. Three attempts were made to fire a lifeline towards him. At the third attempt he grabbed the line and made it fast so that a breeches buoy could be run out to the trawler. The survivor pointed towards the foredeck where, to everyone's amazement, another four men appeared and started waving.

Wrecked at Gwenver 1914

By then the helicopter, which had recovered a body from the sea and transferred it to the lifeboat, arrived over *Jeanne Gougy*. The winchman, Flight-sergeant Eric Smith, lifted the five men to safety. Although it seemed that there was no-one left alive on the wreck, Flight-sergeant Smith and Mr Bridger were still not certain and the RAF man made another search, this time going beneath the deck of the dangerously flooded trawler for a final check. There were no further signs of life.

Later Flight-sergeant Smith, who was subsequently decorated for his gallantry, said: 'Make no mistake about it, I was dead scared. How anyone managed to survive is beyond me. The sea was washing in, but I walked as far as I could through the ship, shouting, but there was nobody alive there.'

The terrifying story of the survivors' ordeal was told by one of them, Michel Pade: 'Soon after she struck, the ship heeled over on her side. Eight men on the balcony side of the wheelhouse were washed away instantly. They were drowned. Water poured into our cabin and grew deeper and deeper. So deep that we had to hang onto electric wires to keep our heads clear of the sea. Soon we could only breathe by lying with our heads back and our faces close against the bulkheads.

'Even our faces were under water. For five hours we had to hold our breath for thirty seconds out of every minute. Some of the men could not stand it. One by one they died and soon only two of us were alive in the wheelhouse. We hung on with our dead shipmates banging and thumping around us. Because of the water in our ears we knew nothing of what was going on outside, but I reached the stage that I knew I must get out if I was going to live. I crawled to the wheelhouse window and shouted. They sent me a line from the cliff, but I was too weak and had to wait for the man from the helicopter to reach me.'

'SCARCELY A WORD WAS UTTERED, NOR A SCREAM HEARD'

Although running aground or onto rocks, or even collision, are the main causes of the loss of life at sea, fire ranks highly. Although the presence of water in abundance should mean that fires aboard ship can be easily put out, there are two reasons why this is generally not so. First, water pumped aboard has the perverse trick of putting out the boilers, thus causing the pumps to fail. Secondly, if water is taken on board to fight the flames, and is not pumped out, the ship is in danger of either capsizing or of sinking due to the gallons of water held in her hull. Therefore, instead of counteracting each other, the elements of fire, water and wind have often been seen to unite to create disaster.

At the end of February 1825, the transport ship *Kent* passed to the south west of the Scillies. She was heading for Bengal and China with 364 officers and men of the 31st Regiment; twenty passengers and a crew of 148. Her cargo holds were crammed with ammunition.

She ran into heavy weather and an officer was sent to check that all heavy furniture was secure and that the cargo was safely stored and shored into position. The man had an oil lamp with him. As he went into the ship's spirits hold to make sure that the casks could not break adrift, the ship lurched and he dropped the lantern. The glass shattered, and a stream of liquid flame ran forward and surrounded the casks of spirits in a lethal embrace. Instantly the hold burst into flames.

The troops were quickly mustered as fire parties and used pumps, hoses and buckets of water to try to put out the flames, as well as wet blankets, hammocks and awnings in the hope of smothering the outbreak. As Captain Henry Cobb, master of *Kent*, organised all able-bodied men to join the battle, lady passengers were asked to stay in their cabins. They were told that there was no immediate danger as the spirit casks were surrounded by barrels carrying a massive quan-

Standing into danger

tity of drinking water, and that as long as the wind did not freshen, there was every hope that the outbreak would be contained.

'We ventured to cherish hopes that the fire might be subdued,' a survivor said later, 'but no sooner was the light blue vapour that at first arose succeeded by volumes of black dingy smoke, which speedily ascended through all the four hatchways, and rolled over every part of the ship, than all further concealment became impossible, and almost all hope of preserving the vessel was abandoned.

'In these awful circumstances, Captain Cobb, with an ability and decision of character that seemed to increase with the imminence of danger, resorted to the only alternative now left open to him. He ordered the lower decks to be scuttled and the lower ports to be opened for the free admission of the sea.'

The decision to flood the lower portions of the ship was a double gamble. *Kent* would undoubtedly lose stability and, even worse, the speed of the inrush must inevitably lead to the drowning of those people unable to escape from the lower decks. And so the first victims lost their lives, among them women and children and several men who, stricken with seasickness, were unable to move to safety. At the same time, Cobb received the first news that other people had suffocated after being overcome by smoke.

For a while the position stabilised itself. The flames seemed to be contained; the inrush of water in the lower decks had found a level satisfactory to itself; and almost 600 people were accounted for and safely on deck. Almost unbelievably, the children were the least concerned. 'I was much affected by the appearance and conduct of some of the dear children who, quite unconscious of the perils that surrounded them, continued to play with their toys. The adults were not so composed. While some were standing in silent resignation or in stupid insensibility to their impending fate, others were yielding themselves up to the most frantic despair.'

Almost beyond belief, in so wide an expanse of open sea, help was at hand. Bearing down on *Kent* came the tiny brig *Cambria*, carrying twenty or thirty Cornish miners bound for Mexico. 'For ten minutes or so we were in doubt as to whether she had seen our signals or, if having seen them, she was either disposed or able to help us as she was but one sixth of our size. But she recognized our peril, hoisted British colours and crowded on all sail to hasten to our relief. When I reflected upon the tremendous sea that was running, on the exteme smallness of the brig, and the number of beings to be saved, I could only hope that a few might be saved; but I darest not, for one moment, contemplate the possibility of my own preservation.'

Fearing that a panic rush for the lifeboats might lead to even more casualties, Captain Cobb ordered the passengers to be broken into small groups, each guarded by soldiers with drawn swords. 'Scarcely a word was uttered; not a scream was heard. Even the infants ceased to cry, as if conscious of the unspoken and unspeakable fear and anguish that was in that instant rending the hearts of their parents. Nor was the silence broken, save in two cases where wives plaintively entreated permission to be left behind with their husbands.'

Gradually, and with painstaking slowness, the transfer took place. Some of those aboard *Kent* jumped into the sea and were lost. Others were convinced that they stood a greater chance on the burning transport than on the diminutive *Cambria*, and refused to leave. As the last boats pulled away after twelve hours of gruelling work, it was accepted that all who could be saved, or wished to be saved, had been offered the choice. *Cambria* moved to a safer distance in the hope that she could, if required, still be of help although dangerously overloaded.

With a sudden upthrust of flame, the fire took hold. The seas became alive with the reflection of the blaze. Burning sails disintegrated into a myriad of comets which showered down to give all the impression of a grotesque and immense bonfire night celebration.

'The flags of distress, hoisted in the morning, were seen for a considerable time waving amid the flames, until the masts to which they were suspended toppled over the ship's sides. At last, the devouring element having communicated to the magazine, the long-awaited and long-threatened explosion was seen, and the blazing fragments of the once magnificent *Kent* were instantly hurled, like so many rockets, high into the air, leaving in the comparative darkness that succeeded the dreadful scene of that disastrous day floating before the mind like some feverish dream.'

It was off the Scillies that, on 2 January 1852, another disaster took place when weather and fire replayed their lethal alliance and 161 people perished. The steam packet *Amazon* was outward bound on her maiden voyage to the West Indies. Built at Blackwall, she was described as 'a mighty castle of the deep — the largest steam-driven vessel ever built in England'. Her two 800 horse-power engines needed the attention of twenty-six furnaces to provide the energy to

The steam packet *Amazon* caught fire off the Scillies

drive two massive paddle wheels, each forty-six feet in diameter. In the money of the day she represented a lavish investment of £100,000, and had on board cargo worth a further £100,000 including silver worth £20,000 and a large quantity of explosives destined for the mines of South America.

She was already well behind schedule as she cleared the Scillies, having had to stop twice to allow overheated engine bearings to cool. This was a personal blow to her owners, with a mail contract involved with penalty clauses for late delivery; and a threat to the prestige of her captain who had promised to set up a new record of fourteen days for the 3,622 mile voyage.

She was therefore going flat out when the alarm was given that there was a fire somewhere in front of one of her two funnels. In well-drilled manner, the crew put wet swabs on the deck and engine gratings and played jets of water into the seat of the blaze. As the heat became intense they had to retreat, having to abandon the only deck-pump in their feverish withdrawal.

Fanned by a near gale, the greedy flames ate their way onwards. The master, Captain William Symons, gave orders for the hay that had been packed around the paddle shafts to cut vibration to be thrown overboard. This was done, but by then the fire had reached the huge piles of boiler coal stored at the approaches to the furnaces, and gone on — replenished — to engulf the paddle-boxes themselves.

Although the passengers had gone through a rudimentary exercise on what to do in an emergency, reality was very different to the care-free way in which the drill had been carried out. The boat drill, within hours of sailing from Southampton, had been a carefree and leisurely distraction in good visibility and perfect conditions. Now they were confronted with a real crisis with the alien intrusion of thick smoke and choking fumes. Instead of going to their emergency stations, the passengers blundered about finding each escape route ringed in fire. What little reaction there had been to discipline vanished when, with their clothes ablaze, two screaming people rushed to the side and threw themselves overboard.

Ignoring the officers and crew, the passengers tried to launch the lifeboats. Nine were swung out and lowered, but four capsized in the confusion, spilling their occupants into the rough sea. Death by drowning, death by suffocation, or death by burning seemed the only choice with most of the boats out of action. Men and women in the sea were either swept away or dragged into the vortex of the threshing paddle wheels which kept up their own crazy momentum at increasing speeds as pressure built up in the abandoned boilers.

Some boats were launched successfully, one of them commanded by Midshipman James Vincent. 'As we looked back towards the ship', he said, 'we could see people on her decks. Some were quiet, kneeling in prayer. Others, some of them almost naked, were running about and screaming with fear.'

The end was not long in coming. With a deafening explosion, the ship blew itself apart and sank through debris and floating bodies, taking Captain Symons and many of her crew and passengers with her. Only fifty-eight people survived the disaster out of 162 who had sailed, making their escape in three lifeboats. Two boats were rescued by passing ships within a day or two, but the third — with neither oars, mast or sail — drifted out into mid-Atlantic for ten days before it was spotted by a Dutch ship and brought to safety.

Midshipman Vincent was a key witness at the inquiry into the loss. He revealed that, of the nine lifeboats carried by *Amazon*, four were fitted in such a way that launching could not have been carried out with any degree of safety. Captain Symons, he said, had become almost bemused by the inevitability of disaster and had not even given the order to abandon ship, his last words being 'It is all over with her' in apparent acceptance of his inability to cope.

Those who knew Captain Symons discounted the criticism. He was, it appeared, a gallant and outstanding man who — had he lived — would have received, on his return to Southampton, a silver trumpet as a token of appreciation from the United States Mail Steamship Company for his action in saving a group of American citizens from a large number of armed and infuriated natives. The accompanying testimonial, which he was never to see, referred to his action as being: 'A high display of courtesy, characteristic alike of British honour and humanity. Honourable to the British flag and to his officers and men'.

'SHE LOOKED LIKE A BATTERED TIN CAN'

According to old belief, the ever-present minerals to be found in Cornwall exerted a strange magnetic 'pull' over shipping and thus caused vessels to run ashore. Then, too, were the tales that wreckers lurked on the cliffs, using false navigation lights to attract ships, like moths, to destruction. Both theories were obviously untrue, since science has yet to discover any magnetic force that works on a wooden hull, and historians have yet to uncover a single factual incident in which Cornish wreckers lured a ship to its doom. The wreckers were, in reality, those who took whatever they could find from a shipwreck, admittedly often killing survivors since, under ancient law, a shipwreck was not established while any living soul survived.

It cannot be denied that there was a massive toll which, if reconstructed in orderly fashion, would make it almost possible to walk from the north-easterly point of Cornwall, beyond Morwenstow, to the most south-easterly, beyond Rame, on the ships that have foundered there without once stepping ashore. Indeed, the wreck chart of Cornwall resembles the myriad of bones that run along the outside edge of a huge flat-fish, in an unbroken symmetry of tragedy and loss.

Almost 250 years ago, efforts were made to provide reliable charts by which seamen could keep clear of many of the dangers that lay in the path of the ignorant or the unwary. Captain Robert Heath, wrote in 1750 'concerning the situation of the *Lizard* Point and the Islands of *Scilly*, the late ingenious Doctor *Halley* having remarked that they are laid down in former *Charts* too far Northerly, which Mistake is here corrected'. In very elaborate fashion, Captain Heath drew up his own charts: '. . . that the skilful Mariner may be able to sail with greater Safety in these dangerous *Seas*, I have here inserted a Map, by a diligent Attention to which, he may avoid those Hazards which otherwise he will be exposed to in these Parts of the *Ocean*. And as a further Help to his safe sailing in his *Approaches* to any of these Islands, I have added a Draught of their different Appearances and Aspects from whatever Quarter he views them at sea.

'Ships being sometimes lost on the Coast of *Scilly*, by the Neglect or Misconduct of the Seamen, especially in bad Weather, it is not distinguished that Ships are as liable to be lost on many other Parts of the English Coast if due Care is not taken by the Skilful Mariner.'

Although a soldier, Captain Heath obviously had a shrewd knowledge of the sea. He was correct in that the coastline of Cornwall was, if navigated with care, no more dangerous than that of other parts of the United Kingdom: he was right in blaming indiscipline and alcohol as major causes of disaster; he was accurate in drawing attention to higher standards of seamanship and navigational expertise.

Eighty-six years after the publication of Captain Heath's findings, the Royal Humane Society was told, in 1836, that much of the great loss of life at sea was caused by the ignorance of seamen who were not trained to use the sextant or the chronometer, or in the use of instruments designed to assess the depth of the sea when running near the coast, or amidst reefs or shoals.

In the same year, a Member of Parliament for Sheffield, James Silk Buckingham, was appointed chairman of a Parliamentary Select Committee charged 'to inquire into the cause of the increased number of shipwrecks, with a view to ascertain whether such improvements might not be made in the construction, equipment and navigation of merchant vessels as would greatly diminish the annual loss of life and property at sea.'

Buckingham was an ideal, and experienced, choice as chairman. Born at Flushing, near Falmouth, in 1786, he had a seafaring background and a varied career as traveller, seafarer, journalist and merchant. His Committee found that the losses were due to the bad construction and design of ships; poor repair; inadequate safety and navigational equipment; the bad and unstable loading of cargo; the incompetence of masters; drunkenness amongst officers and crews; poor charts; and a laxity in observing the minimal safety requirements of insurance under-writers.

Drunkenness was given as a frequent cause of the loss of ships and lives, the intoxication of those on board preventing them either giving or responding to, orders in an emergency. Helmsmen and look-outs, it was found, were frequently drunk while on duty, having liberally fortified themselves with alcohol before long spells on

James Silk Buckingham   **Davies Gilbert**

watch. 'Crews', the Committee found, 'sometimes obtained access to spirit casks and, becoming intoxicated, were insubordinate, insolent, disobedient and mutinous.'

Officers were, in the main, inexperienced and often ignorant of their duties and responsibilities. Many could not manage even elementary navigation, whilst those who could navigate often found themselves aboard vessels not equipped either with sextants or chronometers. Captains were frequently young and inexperienced and were sometimes appointed by a shipowner willing to do a favour to a friend by finding a job for a wayward son. The captain of one ship was found to be a lad of fourteen; another was formerly a porter in a warehouse; a third could not only barely write but, on a simple test of navigation, placed his ship several hundred miles off course.

Although, as a result of the report and recommendations of the Buckingham Committee, regulations and requirements were tightened up regarding the competence of officers and the seaworthiness of ships, 36,000 British seamen lost their lives between 1872 and 1884 — a frightening figure equal to one man in six of all those employed afloat over those twelve years. If twenty-four years is

60

taken as the average working life at sea in those days, then one man in three was destined to die in a shipwreck or other loss.

Cornwall played a very important role in the humanity and mechanics of shipwreck. Until 1808, no victim of death at sea could be buried in consecrated ground for fear he was not a Christian. Corpses were either left on the beach in the hope that the tide would reclaim them, or else buried in unmarked graves in deep sand, or in the cliffs, as near as possible to the shoreline.

This uncaring and barbaric attitude — in which a corpse was a liability once it had been stripped of its clothes and anything of value — so incensed a Helston solicitor, Thomas Grylls, that he protested to his Member of Parliament, Davies Gilbert. Gilbert, through the interest and help of the Speaker of the House of Commons, John Abbot (who also represented Helston), introduced an Act of Parliament, in July 1808, which provided that it should be the duty of the local authority responsible for any beach or foreshore upon which a drowned body might come ashore, that the body be laid to rest, with Christian rites, in the nearest churchyard, the cost to be met from the local rates.

In addition to looking after the spiritual needs of the dead, Helston figured in the development of a life-saving apparatus that was to become world famous. When *Anson* was lost off Loe Bar, a young cabinet maker was amongst those on the shore who went through agonies of frustration as attempts to get a line aboard the stricken frigate failed. He was haunted by the spectacle of the dead and drowning and, for several years, experimented with ways of propelling a lifeline over great distances.

In 1816, he perfected a system in which a light line could be fired to a wreck by a muzzle-firing rocket. This line could then be used to pull out a heavier rope from which a canvas harness, or breeches, could be suspended. The main problem to be overcome was that the apparatus had to be small enough and light enough for speedy and easy transport. Using his cabinet-maker's skill and his precise eye, he managed to house the entire equipment in a small chest. Rumour has it that the inspiration for rocket-propulsion came as he watched a firework display.

In June 1816, in the presence of the Mayor of Helston, Henry Trengrouse gave a public demonstration. Four times in succession the rocket carried the line 160 yards across the mouth of Porthleven harbour. On two return runs it carried a man, safely, along a tight-

**Trengrouse demonstrated his rocket apparatus in
Porthleven Harbour**

ened hawser, in a flexible chair. On two more, according to *The West
Briton*, it bore a man 'enwrapped in a float of cork, which encompassed the body, like a pair of stays, without in any measure, impeding the free motion of the limbs'.

But although Trengrouse's apparatus could save men from the
sea, it could still not save ships from the rocks. In 1845, for instance,
it was noted that — in living memory — more than 200 ships had
been wrecked on the stretch of coastline from Trevose to Lundy,
alone, with the loss of at least 426 lives. The toll was probably much
heavier, since many victims would have included fishing smacks and
even smuggling craft and not, therefore, ever reported as overdue or
missing. With 40,000 ships passing along the coastline of North
Cornwall each year, many would have been lost without anyone
being the wiser if, in fact, the owners actually cared.

Many watchers and would-be rescuers might even have felt that
heroism was not worth the risk and the effort, and certainly not the
reward. In 1857, a Lizard fisherman spotted a ship carrying 800

passengers and crew in difficulties as she was swept onto rocks. Without hesitation he climbed aboard, took command, and piloted her out of danger. Although he probably saved scores of lives and a ship with an estimated value of £100,000, he was given £5 by the Admiralty for his help!

In 1874 there was praise for the courage of lifeboatmen from Newquay who, in tremendous seas, rescued the crew of the German barque *Gottenburg*. Conditions were so bad that, not only was the lifeboat flooded, but she was frequently hidden whilst only a few yards from the pier. What made the rescue even more outstanding — 'one of the most gallant ever performed on these shores', it was reported in *The West Briton* — was the fact that the regular crew were so afraid of the conditions that all but two of those who put out were inexperienced volunteers.

Cornish lifeboats have, themselves, been victims of the cruel Cornish sea. In February 1867, the Padstow lifeboat *Albert Edward*, a ten-oared boat named after the then Prince of Wales, was lost with five of her crew of thirteen.

Called to the schooner *Georgina*, she was carried offshore by the wind and tide and she could not get back. She made for Polzeath in the hope of getting shelter. The angry seas caught her and, although her anchors were put out, they could not control her drift. As the crew strained against the sea, four oars broke at once . . . followed by three more. Disabled and at the mercy of the elements, she bobbed like a cork until she overturned throwing eleven of her crew into the sea. She righted herself, and then capsized yet again. As those on shore watched the drama of the men in the sea, *Albert Edward* came upright once more and, unbelievably, came ashore in an undamaged condition.

The year 1900 saw a second disaster engulfing a lifeboat from Padstow. On 11 April, the lifeboat *Arab* went to the aid of the ketch *Peace and Plenty* which was drifting onto rocks off Greenaway, near Trebetherick. Clearing the aptly-named Doom Bar, *Arab* tried to locate the ketch, unaware that it had already been wrecked with the loss of three lives. One colossal wave hit the lifeboat, and broke or carried away nine of the ten oars on which she depended. She was in obvious and immediate danger and her coxswain ordered the burning of distress flares before trying a rescue bid with a million-to-one chance of success. Looking at the hostile rocks, he decided that the best hope lay with getting the disabled boat through them into the

Launching the *Arab* lifeboat at Padstow

comparatively peaceful waters that lay to shoreward of the breakers. Using the storm anchor to slow their rate of drift, he had the four spare oars brought into use and, in the lull between each wave, gingerly directed *Arab* towards a small gap which seemed large enough to let her through. His instincts and seamanship proved correct, and *Arab* came to rest in a fissure in the reef, her crew of thirteen scrambling to safety.

Cruising in the area, and also on her way to *Peace and Plenty*, was the motorised lifeboat *James Stevens No. 4*, under Coxswain Grubb. Seeing a flare from *Arab*, he mistook it as being from *Peace and Plenty*, and changed course. As he started his turn, the lifeboat was struck by a huge wave across the bows with such force as to lift the stern out of the water. The violence of the sea capsized her, throwing seven men over the side, but trapping four colleagues in the engine room. Three of the seven were saved, but eight lifeboatmen died that night including the coxswain and his son. The lifeboat, *The Royal*

Arab **and the trawler** *Peace and Plenty* **on Greenaway rocks**

Cornwall Gazette reported, was washed, upside-down, into a cave where she looked for all the world 'like a battered tin can'.

St Ives was to lose two lifeboats within the space of twelve months, in 1938 and 1939. The first of these was on 31 January 1938 when, in heavy seas, Coxswain Thomas Cocking went to the rescue of the crew of the Panamanian ship *Alba*, at Porthmeor. After waiting patiently until the shipwrecked crew came aboard — having been persuaded, however reluctantly, to leave their personal possessions behind — Coxswain Cocking turned for home with about twenty survivors on board. As the lifeboat, *Caroline Parsons*, came level with the wreck's bow, she was hit broadside by a gigantic wave which threw everyone into the sea within the horrified gaze of relatives and friends who were watching the rescue. The seamen found themselves threatened yet again by the sea they had so recently cheated, but saw the incredible sight of the self-righting lifeboat bob back onto a level keel.

Although eighteen of the survivors, plus the nine lifeboatmen, were able to reach safety, five men from *Alba* were lost. In the ensuing few minutes the lifeboat, totally out of control, ran ashore and became a total loss, with lifeboatmen and seamen alike being rescued by the life-saving apparatus crew and by members of the public who dashed, time and time again, into the surf to help men to safety.

There was, however, to be no safe deliverance when, just under a year later, the new lifeboat, *John and Sarah Eliza Stych*, met disaster while putting out in a hurricane on a rescue bid that was even beyond the launching resources of the lifeboat at Sennen. Winds were gusting to over 90 m.p.h., and the seas were mountainous.

Clearing the shelter of St Ives Head, the lifeboat ran into a very heavy sea. As she began a wide turn to come onto course, she was hit on the bow by a massive wave and capsized, with four of the eight men on board disappearing to their deaths — Coxswain Cocking, acting bowman William Barber, signalman John Thomas, and

North coast victim

Lost off Mawgan Porth 1908

crewman Edgar Bassett. A fifth man, William Freeman, was also thrown overboard but hauled back to safety.

The engine was out of commission. It was started, but stalled and cut out three times. The propeller had become fouled by debris washed overboard at the time of the capsize. With *John and Sarah Eliza Stych* upright once more, distress flares were burned. Another huge sea hit her, and she capsized yet again, this time claiming the life of her motor mechanic, Richard Stevens. Once more she shook herself free and came upright. A few minutes later one of the three men still on board shouted the warning: 'Look out, a big sea coming.' It capsized the lifeboat for the third time, and when she righted herself, William Freeman was the only man still living.

A few minutes later, *John and Sarah Eliza Stych* hit the rocks near Godrevy and Freeman was able to climb ashore. Even then his ordeal was not over, for the angry, clawing sea tried to drag him back to his death as he searched for a gap in the cliffs. Eventually he found it, and returned to St Ives to tell the tragic tale.

Ironically it was never established exactly what ship had been the reason for the launching of the St Ives lifeboat on that tragic night, although it seems likely that it was the steamer *Wilston* which was found wrecked next day with the loss of all thirty-two who had been on board.

Following the loss of two lifeboats within the space of a little under a year, the Royal National Lifeboat Institution closed the St Ives station almost immediately after the funeral and the inquests. Yet, despite the severity of their grief, it was typical of the spirit of the town that, as soon as war was declared in 1939, they pleaded for a chance to operate a new lifeboat. Their request was not denied.

The lighthouse on Godrevy Island today marks the Stones reef

'WITH SEVERAL DEAD, AND ONLY TWO LIVING, MEN UPON IT'

Fate managed two cruel blows against the followers of the Stuart cause that January day in 1649. In London, Charles I took his place kneeling before the executioner's axe in Whitehall. Three hundred miles away, at Godrevy island, in St Ives bay, the vessel *Garland*, loaded with the clothing and effects belonging to the king, and the jewellery of his fugitive queen, was driven ashore in the great storm that, Stuart supporters claimed, showed the wrath of the sea and the wind at the fate of their king.

Garland, bound for France, had sheltered in St Ives bay in a desperate attempt to ride out the worst of the wind and seas. With anchors out, and ropes straining, she fought against the force of the elements threatening to fling her onto the hostile shore. Almost at the very moment that the axe sliced through the king's neck, the anchors parted company with the ship and, like a leaf swept away in a flooded river, she was thrown onto the reef.

It took three days before rescuers could, with even modest safety, approach the wreck. But it was too late. Of a crew of 60, all but two — a man and a boy — were dead. They, together with a large dog, miraculously swam into the lee of Godrevy island and came ashore. For three days, before they were taken off, they lived on whatever rainwater they could catch and whatever seaweed their stomachs would not reject.

Tradition had it that the queen's jewels were washed up on Gwithian beach and were hidden by villagers when soldiers came in search of them. The soldiers may have missed the jewellery, but they did take possession of a few, pathetic, items including 'a scarlet coat with gold buttons, a coverlet, and several pieces of drapery and other linen'.

For two hundred years more, the unmarked reefs of St Ives bay claimed their unrecorded toll of men, ships and cargo. Shipwreck and disaster were so common that it needed to be on a massive scale to win even a passing mention in the newspapers of the day. The loss of *Neptune*, in April 1838, was a rare exception in that the loss of a ship and her crew of nine might not have been recorded, had it not been a tragedy that stirred the hearts of all.

Neptune was a brig of about 170 tons and sailing from Liverpool to Rotterdam with a valuable cargo. So ferocious was the impact with the rocks, and so ruthless the waves, that even experts could not positively identify her from the wreckage that was washed ashore — a mixture of ship's timbers and a cargo of spices, cotton, buffalo hides — and it was only when a boat with the name *Neptune*, and carrying the official documents of her master, Daniel Grant, was washed up that it was accepted that this was, indeed, the wreck. As the bodies came ashore they were collected and, including Daniel Grant and his young son, were eventually buried beside the tower in Gwithian churchyard.

On 30 November 1854, the same stretch of coast saw another disaster as the 700-ton steamer, *Nile*, struck the reef known as the Stones, and everyone on board drowned. *Nile* was a small, but fast, passenger and cargo ship owned by the British & Irish Steam Company. Built at Greenock, in 1849, she worked on a regular schedule between Liverpool and London, calling at Bristol, Penzance, Falmouth and Portsmouth on the way. She usually sailed from the Mersey on a Sunday, docking at Penzance on the following evening.

On what was to be her last voyage, she sailed from Liverpool several hours late, with about forty people on board and an estimated 400 tons of cargo, mostly textiles from Manchester for Cornwall. The estimated value of ship and cargo was in the region of £45,000. In bad weather she headed south, reaching Bristol late but safe. A few hours later, with Lundy to starboard, she was seen heading through worsening weather in the general direction of Land's End as a threatening winter evening turned into the menace of a stormy November night.

What happened next will never be known, but it is thought that either one error took place, or a series of small incidents that culminated in disaster. Possibly the compass became erratic, or engine power was lost or, perhaps, her steering failed. Alternatively, her master, Captain Moppett, might have misjudged the distance he had covered under much reduced speed.

Whatever the reason, the fact emerged that — although still eight-

Gwithian Churchyard where the *Neptune* victims were buried

een miles from Land's End — *Nile* began to swing to the south-west, and ran onto the Deeper Stones, in St Ives bay. Several miles offshore, hidden from the land by driving rain; unable — in the wind — to get a response to her distress maroons, she soon foundered, giving little hope of escape to her crew of twenty-five and their fifteen passengers.

By daybreak all that remained were the inevitable debris of shipwreck. Personal possessions and clothing bobbed alongside casks of butter. Oatmeal mixed with beef, and butter with drapers' cloth. And amongst it all came the bodies . . . a husband and wife married but a month earlier . . . a Mousehole fisherman coming home after two years at sea . . . a maiden lady from Devonport . . . a mother and her child, due to land but a few hours later.

71

Three years later, in October 1857, St Ives was again a town of mourning when the local schooner, *Mary Welch*, running down to Hayle with coal, hit the Stones with the loss of all on board including the captain and his son.

Bude, further up the north Cornish coast, recorded one of its worst disasters in October 1862, with the agonising loss of twenty-four men almost within arm's length of safety. The sailing ship *Bencoolen* had left Liverpool for Bombay on 13 October. She had a crew of thirty-two and a ship's boy, and was carrying a general cargo.

In an unexpected gale, she lost her foremast and sprang a serious leak. Her master, Captain Chambers, reacted in two ways. He took to the bottle, and made for what he thought was Milford Haven — only to find that he was actually approaching Bude. Captain Chambers refused to accept the fact that his navigation was wrong, and would not even come on deck to see for himself the very obvious fact that his ship was being swept across the entrance to the port. *Bencoolen* grounded, broadside on to the seas. The local rescue team

Off Bude 1910

Grounded at Bude

turned out with their rocket apparatus. One shot hit the side of the wreck and bounced off; a second was thrown aside by the waves; a third line reached the ship, but was hurled back by a wave that then swept on to put the lifesaving equipment out of action, cutting off any hope of establishing a direct link from the shore.

Realising the peril, the ship's carpenter tried to swim ashore with another line. Moments later he was dead, engulfed by the boiling waves. A group of volunteers tried to put out in Bude lifeboat, but their courage was greater than their skill and they were beaten back.

Those aboard *Bencoolen* manhandled the ship's raft into the sea. Twenty-seven men clambered onto it, and it swung free. As *The West Briton* reported: 'It was now to be perceived that the raft was quite close to the cliffs on the north side of the harbour; the tide at this time breaking heavily against their base. A little creek, some thirty feet across, at the extreme end of the harbour, was full of fragments of timber, and into this the raft, at last, was washed, with several dead and only two living men lashed upon it. It took but a few minutes to run round the harbour; a line was passed down the cliff, and one by one twelve men, six living and six dead, were drawn and hoisted up, as carefully as could be, rescued with difficulty from a tangled mass of wreck upon the beach, and there laid upon the grass — so fearfully exhausted were those who still breathed, that only one could speak. These were immediately carried to the village. Those who seemed dead were rubbed and rubbed upon the spot, and every man round eager and ready to do his best; one, we thought, gasped, but all exertions were in vain, and they were sent in — dead.

'By this time everything that could break up had broken on the wreck, and was rolling in upon the sands; nothing was to be seen above the water, when the waves were broken, except the black mass of her cargo and a few timbers of her sides. Within two hours from the time she struck, she was in fragments, and twenty-four men had been drowned within a cable's length of the breakwater at Bude.'

The fingers of accusation turned against the local lifeboat crew who, it was said, had failed in their duty to those on the wreck. However, an official investigation found that the only men able to go out were a collection of enthusiastic dockers and other inexperienced men. Even had the Bude lifeboat had an experienced crew, and even had that crew reached *Bencoolen*, only some of those on board might have been saved, the inquiry found. But, with the nature of the storm, the inexperience of the would-be rescuers, and the dangers of the operation, they could not be criticised for their inability to help.

Although the findings on the lifeboat operation were understandable, the attempts to clear the name and reputation of Captain Chambers were not. Despite the claims of many of the crew as to his state of intoxication throughout the hours leading up to the disaster, a campaign was mounted to show him as an outstanding seaman well in command of the situation. Six survivors, perhaps surprisingly, called on a local magistrate to swear an affidavit that Chambers had been sober at all times and that he, and all others on the ship, had displayed the highest qualities of discipline and seamanship. What was surprising about this was that, at the inquest only a few days earlier, they had said — under oath — exactly the opposite.

At the end of October, 1870, the sailing ship *Geneva*, out of Liverpool, was lost with all hands on the Stones, in St Ives bay. It was said that St Ives folk gained benefit to the tune of one hundred cases of brandy, and half as many casks of wine when the sea liberated her cargo. *Geneva*, built in Quebec but three months earlier, was on the homeward leg of her maiden voyage when she foundered.

Few storms created more havoc over a small area than that which was to become known as the 'Cintra Gale', after one of the shipping casualties of the tumultuous hours of 18 November 1893, which claimed three victims off St Ives alone. In a herd of small ships seeking shelter were three colliers, *Bessie*, *Cintra* and *Vulture*. For *Bessie* it was to be a re-run of the night, in 1866, when she had run aground at virtually the same spot. *Cintra* and *Vulture* were both owned by the Cintra Steam Navigation Company, and were carrying coal from South Wales to Dartmouth. *Bessie*, built at Hayle in 1865, was on a voyage from Cardiff to Portland. At first it seemed that they would ride out the storm from the comparative shelter of their anchorages off Carbis Bay. But the wind suddenly changed direction and threw them ashore.

Although St Ives lifeboat was called out, it could not leave the harbour. Neither could it get out of the town by road as the route was blocked by construction work on the West Pier. Fortunately the rocket lifesaving crew were able to make their way to the scene of the three casualties. Although they rescued the entire crews of *Vulture* and *Bessie*, twenty men in all, as well as five from *Cintra*, seven men were drowned.

Aboard *Cintra*, there was little the crew could do as the very anchors on which they were depending became fouled and threatened to pull the ship down by the bows. As the men made frenzied attempts to cut the ship free, they were driven back by the all-engulfing waves which frustrated their efforts. Distress signals were hoisted, and as the ship's boat was swung outwards, it was caught by the wind, toppled by a wave, and capsized, taking with it four men who were amongst those drowned. *Cintra* was thrown onto the beach and those on board jumped to safety, with the exception of one man who stayed on the ship. Minutes later he lost his life as she broke up. The toll of death ended when, within minutes of reaching the safety of land, two other crew members collapsed and died from the effects of exposure and stress.

On another occasion, in January 1895, people on the shore at Portreath had to watch helplessly as, with lifeboats unable to get alongside, the crew of the steamer *Escurial* 'dropped like flies from the rigging into the sea, never to be seen alive again'. *Escurial* was hugging the north Cornish coast when, in a fierce storm, she started shipping water. At first her crew, by manning the pumps, could keep things in check. Eventually water reached the engine room and put the engines out of action as she was swept along the coastline.

She sent out distress rockets while off Newquay, but by the time

**Hayle lifeboat is unable to launch at Portreath to go
to the aid of *Escurial***

the lifeboat was launched, she had drifted down towards Portreath, going ashore on Gull Rock. Newquay lifeboat was recalled and that from St Ives was sent out. By the time they had battled their way through heavy seas to Godrevy, *Escurial* was aground. Due to a mistaken signal hoisted by the lighthouse keepers at Godrevy, the St Ives boat turned back rather than going onward to the wreck. At the same time, a call went out to the lifeboat station at Hayle, and the crew loaded their boat onto a trailer and travelled eleven miles by road to Portreath where, in spite of soft sand, they were able to launch. Minutes later, the lifeboat was thrown back onto the beach and her crew had no choice but to join those on the shore who watched the growing horror that overwhelmed *Escurial's* crew as they climbed to the highest points of the rigging before falling, either from exhaustion or the force of the wind and the sea, to their death.

Miraculously, seven men made their way ashore, and were plucked to safety by rescuers who — in total disregard of their own lives — dashed into the surf whenever anything looking like a survivor could be glimpsed. In spite of this heroism, eleven men died only fifty yards from the mocking safety of Portreath beach.

'NEARLY TWO HUNDRED THUS PERISHED IN THAT DREADFUL MOMENT'

Grief was no stranger to St Mary's. The island's undertakers, for their part, were not without experience in turning unseasoned wood into large numbers of coffins at short notice; its gravediggers were familiar with working in slipping, sandy soil in carving out mass graves for those killed by the sea and then cast up, like broken toys, on the shoreline. But May 1875 brought death on a scale seldom before experienced, and a funeral that seemed endless as almost every cart and carriage was pressed into service in a silent procession in which only the clatter of steel-rimmed wheels over the cobbles disturbed the disbelieving silence of the long day.

Following almost the same route as that of *Association* and her sister ships 168 years earlier, the German mail steamer *Schiller* was closing on Scilly in a lethal combination of fog and darkness on 7 May 1875. One of the finest ships on the run from New York to Hamburg, she was carrying mails, cargo, gold bullion and 254 passengers and a crew of 101. Her general direction was correct with respect to the compass, but she was a short — but critical — distance to the north of where she should have been. Instead of passing to the south of the Bishop Rock, she was travelling at half speed on the inside.

Although the fog obscured the beams of the St Agnes and Bishop lights, those on board *Schiller* should have heard the Bishop's deep-toned fog-bell. They didn't. The first warning of disaster was also the last. *Schiller* moved into the swirling waters that eddy over the Retarrier Ledges. Before she could take avoiding action, she grounded. Her bows went upwards towards the sky while her stern began to disappear beneath the rising waters.

Running aground at low water could not have been worse, since those who thought they had survived the original impact found themselves falling victim to the rising waters which, as they surged and bubbled across the ship and through its rigging, swept dozens to

St Agnes lighthouse when coal was still used

their death each time the scythe of water cut back across the wreck. Distress guns were fired — but were misunderstood by those who heard them. It was a custom of traditional courtesy for liners to fire a gun on making landfall, and to fire another when they had cleared the Scillies, and the distress signals were taken to be courtesies. Lifeboats were washed away before they could be launched.

The angle of the ship increased as the stern dipped and the bows rose, and panic took over. The ship's master, Captain Thomas, tried to reassure his passengers that they would soon be rescued, but they would have none of it. In the rush for the two remaining lifeboats, women and children were elbowed aside as men sought the safety of places. Captain Thomas fired warning shots from his pistol — but he was ignored as the disorderly panic grew. What had been panic grew to mass hysteria as four of the five lifeboats were washed away and the ship's smoke-stack suddenly snapped off and fell among the would-be survivors.

In shocked terms, one of the crew of the Bishop Rock lighthouse wrote to his wife three days after the disaster: 'With heart-sick grief I write to inform you of the dreadful wreck that has happened here, less than half a mile inside us, on Friday night the 7th inst. I had the watch up to eight p.m., when the man who is doing duty here during the absence of the principal keeper took on, but seeing a thick fog coming on I kept in the lantern, and ordered the bell to be set going at 8.40 p.m. — fog very thick. I timed the bell properly at six strokes per minute, and saw that all was right. I left the lantern at ten p.m. and went to my bunk but I could not sleep.

At 11.35 p.m., William Mortimer came running down and yelled to me, and said he could see a vessel on the rocks. I jumped up and went out on the parapet without stopping to dress, and saw the masthead and starboard light of a large steamer. She was burning blue lights and firing off guns and rockets. She seemed to be sinking. The last gun fired was at 1.30 on the 8th inst.

'Fog again raised at six a.m., and I could just then see the topmast of the vessel out of the water. We could count about twenty-six people in the rigging. I could see one lady in the lee side of the rigging with two males by her. She was in a sitting posture, I should think lashed. It was a dreadful sight. At about seven a.m. the mast fell, and I suppose everyone perished, but I still hope a few or some might have been saved.

'On Sunday three bodies floated past us, and this afternoon more

Burying the *Schiller* victims on St Mary's

have passed close to us. No one knows what was felt in this house by all hands to see so many of our dear fellow-creatures suffering and dying so near to us. Their sufferings must have been severe, for it was a cold drizzling rain all night.'

At dawn on 8 December. two rescue gigs put out from St Agnes and pulled five people to safety before they had to return to the safety of shelter. In the meantime, those who had sought temporary shelter behind the deck housing were washed into the sea by a freak wave. 'As they went, a heart-rending cry rent the air,' it was said. 'Groans and cries for help and the long, piercing cries of children were heard for a few brief seconds above the roar of the waves. Nearly two hundred thus perished in that terrible moment.'

By then the highest point of *Schiller* above the swirling waves was the bridge. But even this was not a safe refuge. Each time a wave broke, it dragged its human victims with it. One gigantic sea plucked Captain, Chief Engineer, Surgeon, and a dozen other people into the inevitability of a watery death. Masts and rigging groaned with the weight of those trying to outclimb the clutching billows. Some climbed higher . . . others, overcome with exhaustion, fell into the sea. About half past seven in the morning the iron main mast fell over the side, taking men and women with it and crashing down on the skulls and shoulders of those in its path. Soon afterwards the other mast fell as well in a tearing, splintering arc of death.

At long last help was on its way. The steam packet *Lady of the Isles* arrived on the scene towing the lifeboat *Henry Dundas*. It worked its way through the heartrending jumble of bodies and wreckage, recovering a few survivors, several bodies and twenty-three bags of mail. Of those who had sailed on *Schiller*, only forty reached the safety of land.

For others, like Mr and Mrs Friend, there was to be no safe landing. As *The West Briton* reported, on 17 May 1875, Mr and Mrs Friend 'were enclosed in stout shell coffins lined with lead, and at Falmouth they will be placed in outer coffins and strong wood cases, previous to being sent to Liverpool for shipment to New York.' The newspaper went on to report the recovery of the body of another former passenger by a fishing boat out of Newlyn. 'On being stripped the name of Edward Ball was found marked upon the linen, and it has since been recognised as the gentleman of that name who was on his way to pay a visit to his son in Birmingham after an absence in America of twenty-eight years.'

'THE OFFICERS AND CREW DID ALL THEY COULD'

The standard instructions of the Atlantic Transport Company, Limited, to the masters of its ships were clear: 'The captains are to remember that whilst they are expected to use every diligence to secure a speedy voyage, they must run no risk which by any possibility might result in accidents to their ships. They will ever bear in mind that the safety of property entrusted to their care is the ruling principle which should govern them in the navigation of their ships, and no supposed gain in expedition or saving of time on the voyage is to be purchased at the risk of accident.

'Strict discipline is to be maintained on board, and the captain must see that his authority is thoroughly respected by every officer and man in his ship. He should see that no opportunity is neglected to ascertain the errors in deviation, and the same noted in the compass book for comparison on the next voyage.

'The use of the lead, even if it occasions delay by stopping the engines, is strictly enjoined on all commanders when nearing land . . . and in foggy or hazy weather this will be more necessary.

'It shall be the duty of the captain, at least once on every round voyage, to exercise his officers in a drill by lowering each of the boats overboard, assigning an officer and a certain number of the crew, and exercise them in abandoning the ship.'

In theory, therefore, the rules of the Company; the duties of the captain; the routine checking of position; and the procedures for abandoning ship should have made it unlikely that the steamer *Mohegan* would sink on the Manacles, on the evening of 14 October 1898, with the loss of 106 lives including those of all her deck officers and a stowaway who had been discovered after she had sailed from Tilbury for New York on the previous afternoon.

Built as *Cleopatra*, in Hull, she was sold and renamed whilst still incomplete. Due to a penalty clause for late delivery, work was accelerated to cover a time set-back caused by a strike by her builders. On her first voyage, the shake-down trip from Hull to Tilbury, there was a mishap with one of her boilers. An inspection suggested that there was nothing seriously amiss, and she sailed on her first scheduled run to New York on 31 July 1898. On the way it became obvious that something was indeed wrong with the boilers and when she left New York for London on 15 August, it was ruled that 'owing to the unsatisfactory state of the boilers, no passengers are to be taken on board'. This was a wise precaution since the troubles re-emerged and, in addition, the ship began to leak.

From 4 September until 5 October she underwent a massive overhaul followed by a thorough series of trials under full steam. At the same time her navigating equipment was checked and found to be accurate. All lifeboats were checked. The vessel was pronounced fit to resume her scheduled services and sailed, on 13 October, under the command of Captain Robert Griffiths, the senior captain of the Atlantic Transport Company, Limited. On board were ninety-seven officers and crew; seven cattlemen; and fifty-three passengers. In addition to coal and ballast water needed for the voyage, she had a general cargo including beer and spirits.

About twenty-two hours after sailing, she passed the coastguard signal station at Prawle Point, and gave the customary signal to be passed to her owners: 'All well'. An hour later she was noted passing Rame Head and, as her passengers sat down to afternoon tea, she was seen steaming properly off the Eddystone lighthouse and heading down the Cornish coast on her correct course.

Two hours later, Falmouth coastguards noted coloured lights in the sky in the direction of the Manacles, but it was not until ninety mintes later that they received a message from Porthoustock asking for Falmouth lifeboat, and a tug, to be sent to a shipwreck. There was certainly some confusion when *Mohegan* started to signal that she was aground. An experienced seaman at Falmouth attached little importance to seeing 'a steamer's masthead light, with a bunch of lights, one overhead and some below'. It was, he said, 'a clear night for seeing lights'.

James Hill, coxswain of the Porthoustock lifeboat, saw the steamer standing into danger and, as a precaution, called his crew and launched. By then the steamer's lights had disappeared and although he burned a white light, he received no reply. He was on the point of turning back when 'we fell in with some wreckage, which

was found to be an overturned boat, with two men in her bottom; these were rescued, and cries were heard from beneath the boat. With considerable difficulty we righted the boat, and two ladies, and a child who was then dead, were found and rescued.'

Going on towards the Manacles, coxswain Hill and his crew found a waterlogged lifeboat with a further twenty-four survivors. He took them ashore, obtained a fresh supply of flares, and went back to the scene of the disaster.

'Hearing shrieks and cries I anchored as near the wreck as I could in safety. Quartermaster Juddery, who was in the mizzen rigging, seeing the boat could not approach any nearer the wreck, owing to the heavy tide, swam off to the lifeboat, and, taking a line, swam back again to the rigging, and through his prompt, brave action, materially helped to save the whole of the people in the rigging. The anchor was then lifted and the boat allowed to drop down so as to enable us to take off the rest of the people who were on the rigging and the funnel. The rocks all around were searched, but no other persons were found and, after six hours, the lifeboat returned to the shore two hours before daylight.'

In the meantime the rescue flotilla had been joined by lifeboats

Far left: the steamer *Mohegan* sinking on the Manacles.
Left: her captain, Robert Griffiths.

from Cadgwith and Falmouth, the Falmouth boat having been towed by the tug *Penguin*. By that time the only task left was the recovery of bodies.

It was Mrs Compton Swift, one of the passengers, who first told of the sequence of events that had led to the disaster. About twenty minutes before going into the saloon for dinner, she had noticed the coastline through the twilight, but had thought little of it. 'When sitting down to dinner, and on the point of turning my chair, I heard a crash. The Chief Officer, the Fourth Officer and the Chief Engineer rushed on deck, followed by the passengers. One of the passengers, Mr. Kelly, told me the steamer was aground. Not feeling any alarm, I suggested that we should go back and finish our dinner; when going below, I heard orders given to man the lifeboats, and upon rushing to the stairway, the lights went out. At this time there was a heavy list to port. I heard the captain, from the bridge, give orders. I never at any time felt nervous. The lifeboat, which had turned over, was thrown out into the water, but as soon as it reached the water it righted itself. There would be about twenty-five or more persons in the boat, of whom I was one. After I had been in the boat about two minutes, a wave struck it and turned it bottom upwards.

'Putting up my hands, I thought I was under the bottom of the wreck, but upon realising my position I tried to extricate myself, but was unable to do so as I was jammed between the thwart and the boat. When the boat was righted by the lifeboatmen, one of them by cutting away the wood with an axe, they got me free. I never lost consciousness and was taken ashore. There was another lady under the boat with me and a little child which was dead. The lady subsequently died.' Mrs Compton Swift was convinced that there had been plenty of time for the boats to have been launched. She saw Captain Griffiths on the bridge, and had seen him washed to his death by a large wave.

Another survivor, a Miss Katherine Noble, said that, after the impact, she had been told to keep calm as *Mohegan* had merely grazed something. 'The crew were all rushing to the boats, and I heard someone cry: "Get out the boats". I went back to my cabin to get some wraps, and when I again reached the deck I was horrified to find that no boats had been launched and that the crew were going from one boat to another. Eventually I stepped over the rail to a boat and got in. I heard the captain call out: "Hurry with the boats!". He asked the men why they could not get them out. The men complained that the boats were too full, and the people were ordered to get out, but the crew were unable to swing the boats out. The waves, at this time, were washing over the vessel.

'The Fourth Officer then went to the assistance of some other of the lady passengers; immediately after she was washed overboard and seized hold of some wreckage. She had a life-belt on, the Fourth Officer had not; he was hanging to a hatch close by her for nearly an hour, then a wave washed him away. In my judgment I am sure that the officers and crew did all they could to save the passengers.'

Within ten minutes of striking, *Mohegan* had sunk, with only her funnel and masts left above the level of the waves. For several days the bodies of those who had perished were washed ashore and, in coffins, piled two or three deep while grief-stricken families decided whether to have them buried locally at St Keverne or, at the expense of the Atlantic Transport Company, embalmed and carried home aboard *Mohegan*'s sister ship, *Marquette*.

The cause of the tragic grounding was never established. A Court of Inquiry sat for six days but, with the deaths of all the deck officers, no firm evidence could be presented. The Court found that: 'The captain and officers all having been drowned, we are utterly unable

The memorial to the *Mohegan* victims

to arrive at any conclusion as to why the course was set and steered. We can only suggest that it was done inadvertently by the captain, and from over-confidence on his part he did not discover the mistake in time to avert the calamity. The Court, in conclusion, wishes to express its deep sympathy with the relatives and friends of all the passengers — American and British — and of the master, officers and members of the crew, who lost their lives in this dreadful calamity. Although there was such serious loss of life it is worthy of notice that none of the officers were saved, proving, beyond doubt, the bravery and unselfishness displayed by the master, officers and crew.'

The Court recorded that the 'deplorable loss of 106 lives', only fifty-one being saved, was due to the vessel taking a very sudden and serious list to port, and of there being no light to guide rescuers to her position, or to assist in the act of rescue, the electric light having failed. It recommended that, where a ship was equipped with electric lighting, emergency oil lamps should be available in an easily

Burying those drowned in the *Mohegan*

Gibson
Penzance
Copyright

accessible position.

In recognition of the heroism shown that night, the Court expressed its 'great approbation of the conduct of Mr. Juddery, who, at considerable personal risk, swam from the wreck to the lifeboat, and swam back with a line, and materially aided in saving those in the mizzen-rigging. The Court also wishes to speak with approval of the promptness and skill of the coxswain of the Porthoustock lifeboat, Mr. Hill, and his crew.'

Seven months later another large ship grounded at almost the same point. She was the American steamer *Paris*, with a crew of 370 and 386 passengers on board, and bound from Cherbourg to New York. Travelling at incautious speed in thick weather, she became victim of what was described as 'an unaccountable error of judgment', and ran herself gently aground.

Porthoustock and Coverack lifeboats were soon alongside and stood-by until the tug *Triton* arrived from Falmouth with the Falmouth lifeboat in tow. In an evacuation lasting many hours, the passengers were taken off without incident and a six-week salvage task

The American steamer *Paris* aground on the Manacles

The lifeboat station at Coverack today

started to successfully refloat *Paris*. After temporary repairs, she was taken to Belfast and virtually rebuilt, re-entering service as *Philadelphia*.

Lifeboatmen from Coverack featured in another dramatic rescue, in February 1912, when the German square-rigger *Pindos* was swept, broadsides, onto Chynhalls Point, half a mile from the village, to become a total wreck.

Jim Carey, who was to spend a lifetime in the Coverack lifeboat team, recalled *Pindos* as: 'The worst wreck that ever I was in in all my life. She left Falmouth and she drove ashore here about 8 o'clock in the evening, and she just escaped being destroyed. We launched the lifeboat — a pulling and sailing lifeboat it was in those days — into one of the worst gales that ever I can recall. Using our new gas searchlights we saw her. But we heard her first, grinding herself onto the rocks. We got right in to the scene of the wreck and we got connection with *Pindos*. After a while we got one man off, but the German skipper decided we should call operations off until daylight. We knew we were at risk, but we had to keep at it until all were safe. We couldn't have turned our backs on them and dared to call ourselves men.'

The German square rigger *Pindos*

'PRAY FOR CAPTAIN GREY'

The rocks and reefs off the Isles of Scilly can boast a record of ship-wreck and disaster as endless and as changing as the mighty waves that, even on a quiet day, dash themselves into white and seething eddies of action over ledges that lie hidden one moment, and reveal themselves in open menace the next.

Even in the days of Samuel Pepys, Secretary to the Admiralty three hundred years ago, the Scillies took their toll of ships and sailors. In the early 1660s, 'ye shipe *Royall Oacke*, Mr. Robb Locke, Commander, from ye East Indies is cast away upon ye westerne Rocks of Scilly', according to early records. Then, in the diary of Pepys, for 15 February 1664: 'an extraordinary discourse of the man-ner of the loss of the *Royall Oacke* coming home from Bantam, upon the rocks of Scilly.'

In 1736, the ship *Triumph* 'richly laden, came ashore in a violent storm. This Accident is said to be owing to the ill Conduct of the Crew intoxicating themselves with Rum, at coming into the Sound-ings, and the thick Weather, by the Account of those who escaped', in the words of an official report.

Seven years later an East Indiaman sank in deep water with the loss of all on board. A garrison officer recorded the disaster: 'Their firing of Guns, as a Signal of their Distress, was heard in the Night; but none could give them Assistance. Many of their bodies floated a-shore at St. Mary's and other Islands, where they were buried by the Inhabitants. And some were taken up floating upon the Tide, and were buried.' He was, however, thin on detail regarding the loss of *HMS Lizard*, with over one hundred men drowned, in February 1747.

The year 1784 brought the sinking of the post office vessel *Nancy*, together with her crew and passengers less than an hour after ex-changing signals of goodwill with an American ship. The Americans anchored in St. Mary's sound to await the arrival of *Nancy*. When

**'The rocks and reefs off the Isles of Scilly can boast a record of
shipwreck and disaster . . .'**

she failed to arrive, a search was carried out and wreckage found to
confirm her loss.

The 16 January 1841 edition of *The Falmouth Packet and Cornish
Herald* told of the loss of the steamer *Thames* with a deathroll of
sixty-one after an error of navigation had put her in the midst of a
circle of reefs off St Agnes. 'The ship had only two boats; one was
stove in by a sea, the other some recruits got into it, and lowered her
into the water before any on board were aware of it; two gentlemen
jumped for her, but jumped short, sank, and were seen no more; the
recruits not being able to manage the boat, she soon filled, went
down, and they also soon perished. Thus were sixty or seventy
human creatures left without any means of saving themselves, and
in such a dangerous place, three miles from any inhabited island.'

As the ship settled in the water, those on board climbed up the main rigging until it collapsed, either killing many in the fall, or pitching them into the sea. Listing those who had died, the newspaper added: 'The female was the wife of a soldier, who also perished, as did also the little infant that the mother was suckling . . . Unfortunately for this shipwreck, all the large pilotboats were high and dry when they could have been of vast service; for, had they been afloat, they, in all likelihood would have saved every soul, as they are large enough. It has been a most heartrending shipwreck. The frantic cries of the sufferers could be heard occasionally at St. Agnes.'

As *Thames* settled deeper into the sea, her master, Captain Grey, kept a cool head and showed outstanding leadership, risking his own life to save others. In a letter in *The Times*, a survivor wrote: 'Captain Grey saved our lives, and, what shall I say! I must say! he is gone, he may be alive, but if he is, he must be on the rocks, and if it be pleasing to my good God, may he be spared. May he be spared to his family; his praise is beyond my pen to say that he saved our lives by throwing a rope around us, and then we jumped into the sea. Pray for Captain Grey. I can say no more.'

Two years later saw reports of 'a melancholy wreck of one, if not two, vessels near St. Agnes, Scillies, and no one escaped to tell the sad tale' *The Royal Cornwall Gazette* told its readers in January 1843. 'From a figurehead and other indications, one appeared to be a foreign vessel, but no further particulars can be obtained with respect to her; but fragments of a log book and other circumstances are decisive as to the fate of the *Douro* . . . an inquest was held on two bodies on Monday, one of them no doubt the unfortunate master of the *Douro*, the letters T.G., were imprinted with Indian ink between the fore-finger and thumb of the left-hand.'

Douro, a schooner, had sailed from Liverpool two days earlier on a voyage that should have taken her to Oporto. Only the bodies of the master and four seamen were eventually recovered and buried in the churchyard at St Mary's.

When the Dutch barque *Niekerie* was lost, on 22 February 1844, she was the victim of a strange ricochet impact. She hit one rock, rebounded virtually unscathed and then, at reduced speed, hit another. The 'ripple' effect of the double impact literally shook her to pieces so quickly that eight of her crew were drowned instantly, and only eleven men survived. 'The crew', according to *The Royal*

Cornwall Gazette, 'consisted of nineteen persons, two of whom, namely Simon Greeve, sailmaker, and Christian Soupe, seaman, are saved. Three of the dead bodies have been picked up and buried, but there is no chance of any more of the poor fellows being found. No part of the cargo will be saved, nor any thing of the vessel or the material worthy of notice.'

Greeve and Soupe told a sad story. Although they, and nine shipmates had escaped from the wreck, and made their way to an uninhabited island, all but themselves had died in the hours immediately following the tragedy, either in attempting to swim to safety, or due to a combination of coldness and hunger.

There was only one survivor after the Italian ship *Il Primo* struck the Seven Stones reef in June 1871, and sank immediately. The man saw other crew members drift by, but out of reach, lying across the bottom of the capsized dinghy as he tried to keep afloat by clinging to the wreckage. He was convinced that he would die and that they would be saved. He was wrong. Although the currents eventually

Minnehaha **wrecked on the Scillies in 1874**

swept him ashore between St Martin's and Nor Nor, the wind blew his compatriots out to sea. No other survivors ever came ashore.

As *The Times* of London, put it: 'With reference to the wreck of the ship *Minnehaha* on the Scilly Islands, on Sunday last, it is manifest that no assistance could have been rendered to the unfortunate persons who perished on the occasion.' The loss of *Minnehaha*, together with ten of the twenty men on board, was as the result of confusion over her position — despite the presence of an experienced pilot — and a fatal misunderstanding when the pilot gave one instruction to the helmsman at the very moment that the master gave a totally contradictory order.

Early on the morning of 18 January 1874, *Minnehaha* was sailing in heavy seas and very bad visibility. When a light was spotted, the pilot assumed it to be the Wolf and reckoned that he would have a stretch of open sea ahead of him before approaching the Scillies. It was, however, not the Wolf but the light on St Agnes. Almost immediately, land was sighted and the four-masted barque collided with Jolly Rock.

'It would appear that the port bow was stove right in, for the water poured into the vessel in a perfect deluge and within two minutes she was almost under water,' a survivor said. 'A scene of terrible confusion ensued and those of the crew who had not been overwhelmed rushed into the tops. Among them was Captain Jones, who reached the mizzen-top in safety, and who determined to swim ashore for assistance. He took off his clothes for this purpose but through some cause, probably by becoming chilled, relaxed his hold and fell into the sea, and nothing more was seen or heard of him.'

The official inquiry into the wreck found that, following the confusion between the two lights and the look-out calling 'There is land to leeward', the captain cried 'Put the helm down' at the same moment the pilot ordered 'Put the helm up'. Before the helmsman could react, the ship was aground. It was recorded: 'Had the crew all got into the rigging, and waited till daylight, they would all have been saved; but, as is frequently the case, in the great alarm efforts were made to get ashore, and not seeing where they were going, it leads to fatal accidents. When the masts stand, it is much safer to remain by the ship until daylight.'

The first knowledge that Scillonians had of the loss of the three-masted brigantine *Catherine Griffiths*, at the end of 1875, was when an upturned boat carrying her name was washed ashore. *Catherine*

Griffiths had been launched only a month earlier, and was on her maiden voyage from Sunderland to Rio de Janeiro with a cargo of coal. Her journey had been hampered by fog.

When the boat was discovered, searchers went to the Western Rocks as being the most likely scene of any mishap. 'Eventually a poor fellow who was in a sad state of exhaustion, and who turned out to be the only survivor, was discovered on some rocks', it was reported in *The Royal Cornwall Gazette*. He told them that, in the fog, the ship had hit the rocks head-on and begun to sink. 'Seven men got into the longboat which was jammed between the mizzenmast and the rigging. The survivor, Morgan, got into a small boat with two others, but they died from exhaustion in the water-laden boat, and he had to throw the bodies overboard as they were bumping against him. He drifted ashore and crawled up the rocks to the place where he was found.'

Morgan said that, at first, it was thought that the damage to the ship was trivial 'but soon after it was seen that she was sinking . . . she sank very quickly . . . I waited until the last minute when I jumped overboard. Almost immediately the ship sank with the seven hands on board; all disappeared at once, longboat and all; and no sound whatever was heard. I joined the ship's boy and the boatswain in the small boat. The boy soon began to get weak, and moaned in his despair, but he helped to get the boat righted and got in her. The poor lad, however, fell away on the gunwale, upset the boat and was drowned. We righted the boat but, in about two hours, the boatswain fell away and was drowned. The boat was again capsized and it took half an hour to right her. I got very cold and cramped, and despaired of escaping the fate of my late companions.'

For two hours, on 22 June 1901, the four-masted barque *Falkland* fought a desperate battle against wind and tide in an attempt to clear the Bishop Rock. After clearing the Bishop, the master found his course barred by a reef he had not seen in his earlier manoeuvre. It was as he tackled this new threat that his ship was swept back to her doom. *Falkland* scraped the rocks, tearing out her bottom, and was surged onward into deeper water. In the process she came so close to the Bishop Rock lighthouse that her yards actually scraped the side of the lighthouse as she passed. Although one boatload of

Bishop Rock lighthouse today ▶

survivors reached safety, the second — which contained the captain and five men — was dragged to the sea's bed as the barque sank under them. The disaster was watched by twenty-seven people in the longboat, who included the captain's wife and child.

Thomas W. Lawson was a unique ship. The graceful seven-masted schooner was the first and last of her kind, and was described by many as one of the finest ships of her day. She displaced almost 5,000 tons, had an overall length of 375 feet. Her sails, when stowed, weighed eighteen tons. When fully displayed, they had an area of 43,000 square feet. Designed to operate with great economy, she carried a crew of only eighteen.

On the afternoon — perhaps significantly — of Friday 13 December 1907, she approached the Scillies in a heavy gale. She was enroute from Philadelphia to London with a cargo of 2,250,000 gallons of oil. According to *The Illustrated London News* of 21 December 1907, the captain found himself too close to the islands. 'There was no room to wear ship and there was not sail enough to tack. The ship

Reconstruction of Bishop Rock lighthouse, 1887

Thomas W. Lawson, **a seven-masted schooner**

was, therefore, brought-to and anchored. Her position was dangerous. She was in waters teeming with rocks and submerged ledges.
With two anchors out, she faced the fury of a fierce north-west gale.
Accompanying the gale were mountainous seas, and the ship could
not have been in a worse position.'

As a precautionary measure, the lifeboats from St Agnes and St
Mary's went to the American ship and offered to take off the crew or
stand by. This was politely turned down by the master, Captain
George Dow. He agreed, however, to take one of the St Agnes lifeboatmen — Mr William Cook Hicks — on board when he discovered
that Hicks was a qualified pilot.

Throughout the Friday evening and into the night, a watch was
kept from the shore on the lights of the giant schooner. When, at
2.30 on the Saturday morning, they disappeared, it was assumed
that her lighting had failed. Little did the watchers realise that

Thomas W. Lawson had already gone to her doom and that Hicks was dead, together with all but three of the crew. Unable to stand the force of the hurricane, the anchor cables had snapped and the schooner broke adrift to the fury of the storm.

The Illustrated London News reconstructed the position: 'It was a desperate and awful time. The engineer, Edward Rowe, of Boston, was by the side of the pilot, and when the huge craft trembled from end to end as she was hurled against the rocks, he asked Hicks if there was a chance of getting ashore. Hicks knew every inch of that treacherous part, and replied: ''No''. But, strangely enough, that engineer is one of the survivors. Hicks, to the regret of all Scillonians, is missing and is undoubtedly dead. The end of the ship came swiftly. She only struck once more, and came to destruction. Masts and rigging crashed into the sea and the stern was cut right off. The cargo was freed, and thousands of gallons of oil poured out on to the sea. Every man had a lifebelt, but nearly all were either dragged down in the rigging, dashed against the rocks, or perished in the horrible masses of oil.'

In addition to Rowe, only two other men reached the safety of land. One of them, Able Seaman George Allen, died from severe internal injuries. The other survivor, Captain Dow, was actually brought to safety by Mr Frederick Cook Hicks, the son of the dead pilot, and who swam through a deep gully between two reefs to take out a line in an act of outstanding gallantry which was later recognised by the award of the Silver Medal of the Royal Humane Society.

'UNFIT TO WITHSTAND THE NORMAL PERILS WHICH SHE MIGHT EXPECT TO MEET'

There could hardly have been a greater contrast between those involved. At Truro, in the cold and blustery days of December 1966 and January 1967, sombrely-dressed men carrying charts, diagrams and bulging briefcases made their way into the chilly gloom of the old council chamber in the former County Hall where, facing blanket-draped tables, they heard a long catalogue of facts and qualified expert opinions from a succession of witnesses.

The contrast was with Mylor, and its sunny creek, on the morning of 31 July 1966 when jackets, jeans and swimsuits were the order of the day, alongside picnic baskets, haversacks and all the impedimenta of a carefree boat trip along the Cornish coast.

The link between Truro and Mylor was the motor vessel *Darlwyne* which disappeared on that fatal day, taking with her all thirty-one people who had embarked in such gaiety on a voyage that ended in disaster.

Darlwyne was an elderly craft and had seen several changes and facelifts in her inconspicuous career. She began her days at Shoreham, Sussex, in 1941 as a 45-foot Admiralty medium-speed picket boat. In those days she had no name — merely the service number 41768. After a very dreary time running Royal Naval ratings ashore or back to their ships, she eventually found her way into the catalogues of Government Surplus Sales, and thus to a Southampton boatyard where she was converted into a cabin cruiser. As part of the conversion, all the original bulkheads were ripped out and replaced by four that were certainly not watertight. Four years later her original engines were replaced and she was taken to Teddington, on the River Thames, to begin her life as the 12-ton cabin cruiser *Darlwyne*

Her new owners sailed her to St Mawes, in 1962, and put her up for sale, at Mylor, in 1963. In the following year, in a rather derelict

Mylor Creek from where the *Darlwyne* put to sea

and shabby condition, she was sold yet again. Once more she underwent structural change, but this time at the hands of non-professional owners who sought no advice as to the effects of the various changes that had been, or were being made, on the safety and stability of the vessel. Although there was no obvious reason to doubt her seaworthiness, there were no grounds for taking it for granted. In fact several of the changes that had taken place would make her reaction to bad weather unassessable.

Throughout the summer of 1966, *Darlwyne* was used for cruises without incident. Although she did not carry flares, buoyancy equipment or safety apparatus, she had a small dinghy normally carried aboard; a 16-foot dinghy used as a tender for ferrying passengers ashore; two circular lifebuoys and, possibly, two non-inflatable lifejackets.

Darlwyne left Mylor Creek on the morning of 31 July 1966 with a crew of two and twenty-nine passengers. She was bound for Fowey, despite weather reports that winds would become moderate to fresh and rather gusty along her route. She reached Fowey without incident and, about three hours later, started her return journey. Between 5 o'clock and 6 o'clock various people recalled seeing a vessel resembling *Darlwyne* heading towards Dodman Point. At the time the weather, as forecast, was worsening with maximum wave heights of about six feet. Within two hours, the wind had freshened still further and maximum wave heights had doubled.

Late in the evening it was realised that *Darlwyne* was overdue and was not on her moorings. Telephone calls were made to coastguard stations between Fowey and Falmouth and it was established that the vessel had disappeared and was not sheltering either inshore or in harbour until the weather improved. Throughout the night anxiety grew and, at first light on 1 August, Falmouth and Fowey lifeboats

Old County Hall, Truro, where the Court of Inquiry into the *Darlwyne* disaster was held

put to sea. Ships in the area were asked to keep a close look-out. A helicopter search began; a Royal Air Force Shackleton search and rescue aircraft took off, and the warships *Fearless* and *Ark Royal* became involved.

During the day a dinghy, similar to the one towed astern, was found. Despite bad visibility, the air search continued on 2 August and the lifeboats from Salcombe and Coverack put to sea to widen the search area.

On 4 August the first bodies were found, with others coming to the surface until, by 16 August, the sea had given up twelve of her victims. Each of them had drowned in deep water, the pathologists found. Forensic experts, analysing the type and sturdiness of watches on the victims' wrists, estimated the approximate time of death and — from it — the likely scene of the wreck. Although the Royal Navy located 912 underwater objects in the search area, and divers investigated 142 of them, *Darlwyne* was not found.

By estimating the time and distance of drift of bodies and other wreckage; the cause of death; the time that the watches had stopped; and the evidence of people who had seen the vessel resembling *Darlwyne* after she had left Fowey, the Court of Inquiry was able to satisfy itself that 'the most probable place of the loss is the area off Dodman Point, and the most probable time about 2100 hours on the 31st July.'

Having established the most likely time and place, the Inquiry next had to establish probable cause of the disaster. Noting that one of the bodies, that of a lady, was wearing a jersey that was too large for her, possibly her husband's, as well as a lifebuoy, the Court considered that this might indicate that there had been some general anxiety on board before the vessel actually foundered. This, they thought, was consistent with engine failure and the possibility that she was drifting. Were this so, then those aboard would have taken shelter in the wheelhouse or cabin. Had a heavy sea from astern swamped *Darlwyne*, causing her to sink rapidly, then the theory would take in the fact that all the bodies recovered had died at about the same time, and from drowning in deep water rather than shallow water as would have been the case had she run aground or capsized.

Witness after witness contributed to the bizarre jig-saw laid before the Court of Inquiry. *Darlwyne* had never been surveyed for a Passenger Certificate, it was revealed. Shortly before the accident, an expert had noted that her timbers were possibly rotten, were disturbed and possibly cracked. There was the possibility that unsecured ballast could have moved, thereby endangering the safety of the vessel. Finally, there was the damning opinion that although *Darlwyne* was originally well designed and of good hull form, she was not possessed of sufficient stability or weight-lifting ability to make a voyage at sea in the weather conditions with thirty-one people on board.

Reaching its conclusion, the Inquiry observed: 'The woefully inadequate supply of life saving appliances may not have contributed to the loss of life especially if, as seems probable, everyone on board the *Darlwyne* was in the wheelhouse and cabin and the vessel, at the end, either foundered or capsized. The lack of distress signals may have done so if, in fact, there was trouble with her engines or steering gear. That, however, is not sufficient to establish a causative wrongful act or default. The Court is satisfied that the major cause of the disaster was the *Darlwyne* going on a voyage to sea when she was physically unfit to withstand the normal perils which she might expect to meet.'

ACKNOWLEDGMENTS

The Author would like to express his very sincere thanks, for their great assistance, to the Cornwall County Librarian, Mr John Farmer, and the staffs of the County libraries at Falmouth, Truro and Redruth; to Mr H.L. Douch, of the Royal Institution of Cornwall, Truro; to the staff of the House of Commons Library, and to the Record sections of the Department of Trade and the Ministry of Defence, as well as those at the Public Records Office.

PLATE ACKNOWLEDGEMENTS

Front cover, Paul Broadhurst
Page 5 Ministry of Defence
Pages 8, 9, 31, 32, 50, 66, 84, 90 Osborne Studios
Pages 7, 29 lower, 80 lower, 88, 89, 94, 96, back cover
F.E. Gibson
Pages 17, 19, 21-25, 29 upper, 36, 38, 62, 71, 87, 91, 106, 107
The Author
Page 64 Royal Institution of Cornwall
Page 100 F.E.Gibson, by courtesy of Trinity House
Page 65 Royal National Lifeboat Institution
Page 47 Richard Brothers
Page 48 J.H. Bottrell
Page 43 R.T. Pentreath
Page 68 Ray Bishop
Page 10 Helyn Mudd

SOURCES CONSULTED

S. Baring-Gould, *Cornish Characters & Strange Events*, Bodley Head.

D.B. Barton, *Life in Cornwall*, D. Bradford Barton.

Clive Carter & Richard Larn, *Cornish Shipwrecks*, Pan.

Terry Coleman, *Passage to America*, Hutchinson.

A.G. Course, *The Merchant Navy*, Muller.

Rex Cowan, *Castaway and Wrecked*, Duckworth.

Robert Heath, *The Isles of Scilly*, Frank Graham.

Daphne du Maurier, *Vanishing Cornwall*, Gollancz.

David Mudd, *Cornishmen and True*, Frank Graham.

Jill Newton, *The Lizard*, Bossiney Books.

Cyril Noall, *Cornish Lights and Shipwrecks*, D. Bradford Barton.

Cyril Noall & Grahame Farr, *Wreck and Rescue Round the Cornish Coast*, D. Bradford Barton.

Samuel Pepys, *Pepy's Diary*, George Newnes.

F.N.L. Poynter, *The Journal of James Yonge*, Longmans.

Stanley Rogers, *The Book of the Sailing Ship*, Harrap.

Frank Strike, *Cornish Shipwrecks*, F.E. Strike.

Files of: The Cornish Echo, The Cornishman, The Falmouth Packet, The Illustrated London News, The Royal Cornwall Gazette, The Sherborne Flying Mercury, The Times, The West Briton.

OTHER BOSSINEY TITLES BY DAVID MUDD

CORNWALL & SCILLY PECULIAR

48 photographs.

David Mudd uses his perceptive eye and his pride of all things Cornish to write entertainingly, at times with humour, but always affectionately, of some of the people, events, values and beliefs that create the background to Cornwall's strange and compelling charm.

'... one of the most important Cornish titles produced by Bossiney ...'

The Cornishman

DOWNALONG CAMBORNE & REDRUTH

44 photographs.

With a mine of magnificent old photographs and some presentday ones by Ray Bishop, David Mudd charts the history of the two towns from the 12th century to the present. 'I like a good meaty story,' he says, 'that has an accent on the curious, the bizarre, or even the macabre.'

'His journalist's eyes and ears and his sympathy add to the reader's understanding.'

West Briton

'... spicy but informative ... extremely good value.'

Robert Jobson, Camborne-Redruth Packet

THE CORNISH EDWARDIANS

by David Mudd. 66 photographs.

David Mudd exposes the squalor, the success, the pride and the poignancy, the fun and the futility that shaped Edwardian Cornwall.

'... rich harvest of illustrations.'

Cornish Life

CORNWALL IN UPROAR

by David Mudd. 60 photographs.

David Mudd turns the pages over an unruly Cornish past: miners fought farmers, clayworkers did battle with police, merchant seamen clashed with the Royal Navy and fishermen turned against colleagues from the East Coast. There were protests against the loss of the Roman Catholic faith, unrest if religion was too high or too low.

ABOUT THE CITY

44 photographs.

David Mudd takes a look at Truro, telling of ancient charters, the Civil War, of rivalry with Falmouth, of law and order, fun fairs and funerals, of pills, policemen and stage coaches. There are even fleeting glances of pirates and smugglers. As the author proves, it is not only 'fresh, pure, running water' that flows through Truro. A lively history and a unique atmosphere gush through its streets as well.